D0672331

Presented To:

From:

Date:

ULTIMATE
HINDSIGHT

ULTIMATE HINDSIGHT

wisdom from

100

SUPER ACHIEVERS

JIM STOVALL

Sound Wisdom

P.O. Box 310

Shippensburg, PA 17257-0310

Cover design by Eileen Rockwell and Kelly Morrison

For more information on foreign distribution, call 717-530-2122.

Reach us on the Internet: www.soundwisdom.com.

ISBN 13 HC: 978-0-7684-0961-1
ISBN 13 TP: 978-0-7684-0990-1
ISBN 13 Ebook: 978-0-7684-0962-8

Stovall, Jim.
    Ultimate hindsight : wisdom from 100 super achievers / Jim Stovall.
        pages cm
    Includes bibliographical references and index.
    ISBN 978-0-7684-0961-1 — ISBN 978-0-7684-0962-8 (ebook)
    1. Success. 2. Fame. 3. Fortune. I. Title.
    BF637.S8S69977 2015
    170'.44—dc23

                                                                2015029996

For Worldwide Distribution, Printed in the U.S.A.
1 2 3 4 5 6 7 8 / 19 18 17 16 15

CONTENTS

INTRODUCTION

BY JIM STOVALL

My Dear Reader:

This book has been over a quarter of a century in the making. I have long believed that success in every area of life is a question of following the leader. Once you decide to, indeed, follow the leader, the question becomes which leader you should follow. I am convinced there is not just one right answer to this question.

Gandhi said that everyone is my superior in that I can learn something from them. There are things we can emulate in the most despicable among us, and there are elements of the lives of the elite that we would not want to model in our own lives.

I have written over 30 books, and at this writing, four of my novels have been turned into major motion pictures with several others in production. I have written a weekly syndicated column for almost 20 years read by countless people throughout North America, Europe, and Asia. I am the founder and president of the Emmy Award-winning Narrative Television Network, which has been my main focus for over 25 years.

For several years after NTN began, I hosted a talk show that preceded each of our movies in which I interviewed some of the biggest stars from movies, television, and the Golden Age of entertainment. I have spoken to several million people in business conventions and arena events around the world, which has given me the opportunity to share the stage with some of the greatest achievers of the 20th, and now the 21st, century.

Each of these experiences has given me the opportunity to observe fame, fortune, and success from a unique perspective. There are many celebrities I wish I had never met as their life is little more than a smoke and mirror façade that covers up the empty and hollow existence inside. There are other stars, leaders, and super achievers I wish everyone could know at a personal level as I do. As bright as their public persona shines, the real person inside has even more to offer to us all.

In these pages, you will meet over 100 of these individuals who have determined what is important to them in their lives, and they have risen to the top. While it is fun to stargaze and rub shoulders with the rich and famous, my purpose in writing *Ultimate Hindsight* is to give you the tools that these people have developed over their years of struggle, trial, and error.

If you want to get to the top of the mountain, don't ask someone standing in the valley idly gazing at the summit. Ask someone who has been to the mountaintop or resides there now.

I hope this book is interesting, entertaining, and compelling, but more importantly, I hope it helps you to think about what you have learned from your past along with the hindsight of others that you can bring into your performance today so that your future can be everything you want it to be.

Success is never a destination. It is always a journey, and the journey never ends. Once you reach one mountaintop, you can celebrate your victory as you look behind you and revel in the fact that you have come so far; but while you're standing on the mountaintop, you will also see bigger, taller, and more beautiful summits ahead of you that will beckon you toward them.

Any time I can support, encourage, or motivate you along your journey, I can be reached at Jim@JimStovall.com. I am grateful to you for joining me in this journey within these pages and beyond.

JIM STOVALL
2015

ULTIMATE
HINDSIGHT

Eddie Albert

PUT OTHERS FIRST

TO GENERATIONS OF CLASSIC TELEVISION VIEWERS, EDDIE ALBERT is fondly remembered as "that guy with the pig on the *Green Acres* TV show." If that is all you know about Eddie Albert, you missed a lot.

There are many celebrities who have little substance outside of the activity or pursuit that made them famous. The better I got to know Eddie Albert, the more impressed I became with him as new facets of his personality and achievements were revealed.

I had the privilege—on three separate occasions—to interview Eddie Albert: once via telephone, once in our studios in Washington, DC, and the most memorable time for me when I interviewed him in California in a wonderful garden behind his home.

As our crew was setting up all of the lights and various equipment necessary to do a network television interview, I was casually chatting with Mr. Albert. He was describing all of the flowers and plants in his garden that would be the backdrop for our on-camera conversation.

The sound engineer approached me and told me they were hearing some loud music from the other side of the wall behind the garden, and the noise was being picked up by our microphones.

When I explained the situation to Mr. Albert, he asked his assistant to bring him a portable phone, and he dialed a number from memory. I'll never forget him speaking into the telephone. "Rod, you know we all love your music along with everyone else in the world, but for right now could you just turn it down? Thanks. Good-bye."

I hadn't been paying attention to the music as I had been focused on Eddie Albert and our pending interview, but I was curious about his neighbor. I think Mr. Albert sensed my curiosity and explained, "Rod Stewart is a good friend and a good neighbor, but sometimes he plays his music too loud."

I was struck by the fact that these two performers from opposite ends of the entertainment spectrum had found friendship and cameraderie over the years as they had become good neighbors.

Many celebrities I have interviewed were difficult and hard to deal with. It's the kind of situation that almost makes you wish you had never met them because they aren't always the person whose work you had enjoyed on the screen. Eddie Albert, however, was everything I had hoped he would be and more. I am proud to say that I considered him among my friends. He was a gracious individual. Let me give you an example.

When we arrived at his home for the interview, we had all of our luggage with us so we could go directly to the airport after the taping. When we had completed the interview, the crew was tearing down the equipment and packing up to leave, and Mr. Albert, then 87 years old, carried my suitcase to the front door. I was, in a way, shocked and embarrassed, but I told the crew afterward that I wished we had footage of Eddie Albert carrying my suitcase!

Eddie Albert sang lead with the San Francisco Opera and had given critically-acclaimed performances of Shakespeare's work on the stage. He starred in many motion pictures and received an Academy Award nomination, but to most of us, he will always be Mr. Douglas, the city lawyer who found happiness (and frustration) on *Green Acres*.

During the interview, Mr. Albert had a refreshing way of looking at his work and his life. He said:

> *I really don't care how I am remembered as long as I bring happiness and joy to people.*
>
> *The most important thing to me is the relationship with my family, my long and successful marriage in a town and industry not known for long and successful marriages, and the friends I have developed in and out of the business who know they can trust my work.*

Few people know that Eddie Albert was a decorated hero of World War II. In a daring, courageous effort, he saved a lifeboat full of servicemen who otherwise surely would have perished. Once a year, every year, those servicemen whom Eddie Albert saved put on a banquet to honor him. During my last interview with him, he had just returned from this annual event, and he was most proud of the fact that the men he had saved and the members of their families who attended the banquet then numbered more than 300 people.

Sometimes you do the right thing, and it makes a difference not only at that moment in time but for generations to come.

ULTIMATE HINDSIGHT

Steve Allen

IDENTIFY WITH THE AVERAGE GUY

WITHIN THE ENTERTAINMENT INDUSTRY, THERE ARE FREQUENT stories and rumors about shifts among the late-night hosts. Every time I hear about the projected future of one of these late-night hosts, I always remember the day I got to meet and interview the legendary Steve Allen.

The interview was conducted in Steve Allen's office adjacent to a Hollywood studio. At that time, he was working on his 32nd book and a new CD of original music. Few people know that in addition to his work on television (as the creator and host of *The Tonight Show*) and his work as an author and a television and movie actor, Steve Allen was one of the most prolific songwriters who has ever lived. He wrote more than 5,000 songs and has a Grammy Award to his credit.

I remember arriving at his office that morning with a crew of six. We were told to set up in Mr. Allen's office for the interview. He was writing at his desk when we came in. I asked if we would bother him with the noise and activity from the crew setting up. His assistant told me, "He won't even know you're here." During the half-hour of setup, Mr. Allen continued to work on his book and, when it was time to talk with me, he did a tremendous interview. One of the true secrets to Steve Allen's success, I feel, was his total focus on what he was doing at the moment.

During the interview, I asked him if there was one thing to which he would attribute his success. He said:

> *Whether it's a TV show, a movie, a book, an album, a personal appearance, or an interview like this, I never forget there's a guy at home who is my audience. He is my customer, and I try to come to him on his level and treat him as I would like to be treated. I have never considered myself a star, but instead, just the average guy's embodiment who works in show business.*
>
> *I hope to give people the impression that if Steve Allen can do that, anyone can because that is certainly the case.*

Steve Allen conquered every area of show business and lived a successful life in every way. Many people can say they rose to the top of their field, but few can say they actually created a new field.

The next time you enjoy one of the late-night shows with the latest generation of hosts, remember that it all started with an average guy with above-average talent named Steve Allen.

Dave Anderson

YOU'VE GOT A SPORTING CHANCE

DAVE ANDERSON IS A MEMBER OF THE NATIONAL SPORTSCASTERS and Sportswriters Hall of Fame. He began as a sportswriter for *The New York Times* in 1966. He has also written more than a dozen books, some in collaboration with such sports luminaries as John Madden, Frank Robinson, Larry Csonka, and Sugar Ray Robinson. So you might say that when it comes to observing and learning from the successes and failures of legendary achievers, Dave Anderson has had a courtside seat. And you might expect him to give pages of advice on how to make it to the top. Not so. Displaying his talent for choosing the right words (and not too many of them), this is what he wrote to me when I asked for his comments on success:

> *I don't pretend to tell people how to live their lives other than to do the right thing and work hard. Everything else should take care of itself.*

Sometimes the simplest advice is the best.

ULTIMATE HINDSIGHT

Ed Asner

BEING *THE OTHER*

I FIRST BECAME AWARE OF ED ASNER ALONG WITH MILLIONS OF people around the world when he played the grumpy curmudgeon, Lou Grant, on the hit TV series *The Mary Tyler Moore Show.* He received an Emmy Award for that role, and later, his character was spun off as the lead in the dramatic series *Lou Grant.* This marks one of the few times in the industry the same character has appeared in two different series. Even more unusual was the fact that one series was a comedy and the other a drama.

Mr. Asner is not only a consummate actor but received one of the highest accolades from his peers when he was elected to lead them as the president of the Screen Actors Guild.

At this writing, Ed Asner is in his mid-80s and still working regularly with future projects in development. One might think judging from all of his stardom, accolades, and popularity that Ed Asner was always admired and looked up to. This is simply not the case.

When I asked him to share his hindsight, Mr. Asner recounted the following memories from his early life:

> *I was raised in Kansas City, Kansas. My parents were Orthodox Jews. I was the youngest of five with two brothers and two sisters. My dad owned a junk yard*

27

or what would regally be called a Salvage Reclamation business. When I started second grade, we moved from the Bottoms, as it was called, to West Height Manor, as it was grandly referred to. Quite an economic jump from gazing across the street at Armour's Packing House to a beautiful elm-lined street and a red brick house with a lawn; from my playmates who were Mexicans to white-skinned Anglos; from being one of the smartest in my class to being one of the slowest; from being an only Jew surrounded by Latin and Slovakian Catholics to being an only Jew surrounded by white Protestants.

*Papa's junk business and our Jewishness gave me an intense feeling of being **the other**. My siblings constantly made me resort to euphemisms in talking about Papa's business, and whenever I'd employ them was always found out. One of the boys on my block would get a big kick out of getting his little sisters to sing a song reviling Jews, and I could not retaliate as they were smaller and girls. Such acts constantly occurred to remind me that I was the other. Such acts naturally rankled, especially being blackballed from a fraternity, but in retrospect as I lived in the world, I came to see that these slings and arrows were minor and that they served to make me better, to strive harder to excel.*

*I was well repaid. So I can only close by saying that being the other, that being discriminated in a mild sense, served to make me better, bigger. The phrase **being the other** serves one by making the other strive harder, achieve more. We must be grateful for small disfavors.*

Ed Asner is a shining example of how disadvantages can be turned into advantages. In working with some of the greatest actors in the industry through turning four of my novels into movies, I've gotten to observe these talented individuals doing their magic. I have found that the more life experiences an actor has had and the more situations they have been in, the more they can draw upon as they play their part in a given role.

Ed Asner has seen the world from the bottom up and the top down. It has made him a great actor, a great leader, and a great person.

ULTIMATE HINDSIGHT

Joseph Barbera

BE PERSISTENT

MANY OF US CAN REMEMBER A TIME WHEN "SATURDAY mornings" and "Hanna-Barbera" were synonymous. A generation of children sat glued to the TV set, giggling over the antics of Huckleberry Hound, Yogi Bear, Quick Draw McGraw, Top Cat, Magilla Gorilla, Tom and Jerry, and Scooby-Doo. Adults had their favorites, too, including *The Flintstones* and *The Jetsons*. Who do we have to thank for those timeless shows? Joseph Barbera and his business partner, William Hanna.

I am always intrigued by how people like Joseph Barbera got their start. When I asked him to share his success tips and hindsight perspective, he offered the following:

> *The first job I had was in a bank. At the time, the economy was so bad that I was fortunate to even have work. I didn't really enjoy being an assistant income tax man, so after work, I would create cartoons for magazines to keep myself from going mad. Once a week, I'd go to the magazine offices to retrieve the rejects and then submit new cartoons. Eventually, I sold one and after that, another. With that, I was off and running.*
>
> *Without persistence, it is impossible to experience success.*

Happiness is the real sense of fulfillment that comes from hard work. Winning Oscars brought me an amazing sense of reward, but when I attend gallery openings and see people wait in line around the block for me to sign an animation cel, it adds a joy that is indescribable. I feel fulfilled and honored when parents (at the signings) tell me they grew up on my cartoons and that they enjoy watching them again 40 years later with their kids.

I can't help but wonder here in the 21st century how many people would be pigeon-holed in everyone's single-tracked thinking that a banker or tax preparer could never be a cartoonist or creative genius. Mr. Barbera's tenacity and persistence have brought us all much laughter and joy and will continue to do so for generations to come.

Mary T. Barra

A Woman's World

THERE HAS LONG BEEN A SAYING AMONG ECONOMISTS. "AS GOES General Motors, so goes the economy."

If you had polled leaders in the field of human resources just a generation ago and asked them what positions would be the most unlikely for a female to be offered, most people would have agreed that being the Chief Executive Officer of General Motors would certainly be among them.

Mary Barra began working at General Motors at age 18 when she was a student and worked her way from the very bottom to the very top. I asked her to share some of her hindsight that can help us all get from where we are to where we want to be.

> Don't limit your potential. Sometimes the best learning experiences are the ones you don't expect. When a good opportunity presents itself, make the most of it. Work hard, do your best, take some risks, and always have a positive attitude.

If you want to get to the top at General Motors or anywhere else, all you need do is follow the leaders. Mary Barra is certainly a leader worth following.

ULTIMATE HINDSIGHT

Dave Barry

WHATEVER MAKES YOU HAPPY! (WITHIN REASON)

As someone who's written a weekly syndicated column for almost 20 years myself, I've always been an admirer of people like Dave Barry who keep it current, fresh, topical, and do it well.

You might say that Dave Barry has a unique way of looking at the world, a way of making the incongruities of daily life even more incongruous. Just ask the thousands of newspaper readers who have read his syndicated column. Or you might ask someone who has read one of his many books with titles such as *Stay Fit and Healthy Until You're Dead* and *Claw Your Way to the Top*.

The New York Times once called him "the funniest man in America." He also received the Pulitzer Prize for Commentary. But success hasn't gone to his head—not even when the TV sitcom *Dave's World*, inspired by his writings, was on the air.

What does Dave Barry have to say about success? Let me share with you what he shared with me.

I think success and happiness go together—if you do what makes you happy, you'll most likely be successful.

*(Of course you shouldn't do just **anything** that makes you happy; here I'm thinking of the Unabomber.)*

Vintage Dave Barry.

Ralph Bellamy

DON'T BACK DOWN

RALPH BELLAMY HOLDS THE DISTINCTION OF BEING HONORED with the highest awards that stage, screen, and television can offer. He is among the elite in the entertainment industry who won an Oscar, an Emmy, and a Tony. Many will remember him from the TV miniseries *The Winds of War* and *War and Remembrance*, in which he played Franklin Delano Roosevelt. Or you might have seen him in one of his 107 movies. I had the chance to meet him many years ago.

When I first started interviewing movie stars for our programming on the Narrative Television Network, I was very intimidated, and most of the stars did very little to eliminate my fears. Ralph Bellamy, on the other hand, made me feel welcome and at home and did everything possible to create a perfect interview. He made a career of being the second lead in movies, television shows, and on Broadway, and he had developed the marvelous quality of making everyone around him look good and feel good. I will always remember and appreciate him for doing this for me during our time together.

Mr. Bellamy shared a story with me about his beginnings in show business. I think it applies to all of us.

When I first started in the business, I had no talent, no contacts, and no prospects. My father was an accountant; he asked me to please join him in his business. I told him I wanted to be an actor, and I would never be happy unless I pursued my own goals.

I remember when I got my first part in a play in Cedar Rapids, Iowa. I invited my father to come and see me in this play. As we were walking down the street to the theatre, we passed a rooming house with a sign in the window that said, "Rooms Available. Absolutely No Dogs Or Actors."

My father pointed to the sign and said, "Please join me as an accountant." But he finally understood that being a happy actor is better than being a miserable accountant.

A few years later, I had my own production company. My father's firm failed during the Depression, and I was very proud to have my father as the accountant for my production company for the rest of his career. He was a happy accountant, and I was a happy actor.

And a successful one.

Jacqueline Bisset

ENJOY THE JOURNEY

IN 2013, JACQUELINE BISSET WON THE BEST SUPPORTING ACTRESS Golden Globe Award for her work on the BBC miniseries *Dancing on the Edge*. In 2010, she won one of France's highest honors, the *Légion d'honneur*.

The British-born actress Jacqueline Bisset has never been in a blockbuster movie, but her name and her face are known around the world. Since her movie debut in 1965, her focus seems not to have been on commercial success, but on working when she chose to and doing movies that interested her. At a time when many actresses clamor for attention with exercise videos, books, and products that they sell on the shopping channels, Miss Bisset appears to have chosen a less-congested path. I think that philosophy of a "simpler path" is reflected in her comments to me on success.

> *It is, for myself, very much involved with loyalty and a quiet mind. Sometimes loyalty to oneself, without the endless barrage of self-doubt that we beat ourselves up with, induces a feeling of peace and a realistic assessment of where one really is.*
>
> *To know that one is a good person, thoughtful to others and not petty, is already a great success.*

To be responsible in one's given word to another.

To stand up for good values without trying to control others by force and anger.

To make one's home welcoming to another.

Learning to listen openly to somebody without preparing your response before they have finished.

Taking pleasure in the journey as well as the arrival.

Not living in the future continually or wishing your life away.

Success for most of us has less to do with how we look and sound, and more to do with setting and achieving goals. But as Miss Bisset points out, true success also involves treating others with respect and living in the moment. We can't change yesterday. We can't see tomorrow. All we have is *now.* We should make the most of it.

Pat Boone

ACCENTUATE THE POSITIVE

I INTERVIEWED PAT BOONE ONE DAY AT HIS OFFICE IN LOS ANGELES. This is a man who has done so many things and been around so long we sometimes forget everything that he has done.

On the walls of his office are gold records, movie posters, presidential commendations, and a history of the Boone family showing that he is a descendant of Daniel Boone. It's a remarkable display that documents a remarkable career.

Pat Boone first caught the public eye on a 1950s TV show called the *Ted Mack Amateur Hour*. He wasn't an amateur for long. In addition to his work on television, he forged a successful recording career, appeared in several movies, formed his own record company, and authored a number of popular books. Like most celebrities, he's had his share of failures—some very public—but his faith has given him an anchor in the tough times.

Before our on-camera interview, Pat Boone spent more time talking about and asking about our work at NTN and my books than he spent discussing his own career. I have to say that he is one of the most genuine people I have ever met.

When I asked him what success means to him, he gave me just the kind of answer I would have expected.

41

I define success as somehow having a positive effect on the lives of others.

That includes my own family. It includes my wife, my kids, my grandkids, my friends, the people that I'm associated with. In other words, if I'm involved in any kind of business thing, then I want it to be successful, of course, for those of us who have some major stake or investment in it. But I also want it to have some positive impact on the lives of other people.

So my Easter Seals work, and a number of other either humanitarian or just good old good-neighbor things, are to me as important as the initial career things that I do because it's all part of the same thing. One is sort of the facilitator of the other.

If what you are doing with your life is hurting the ones you love, you will never be able to define yourself as a success. Do what Pat Boone does, and make sure that what you do "for the good of your career" is also good for the people around you.

Jim Brady

LIFE, DEATH, AND LEGACY

BACKSTAGE AT AN AWARDS CEREMONY AT THE KENNEDY CENTER IN Washington, DC, I had a brief opportunity to meet Jim Brady, a man who has a humility and sense of dignity that I have rarely seen in other people I have met. As you no doubt remember, Mr. Brady was the White House Press Secretary. He was with President Ronald Reagan in 1981 during a failed assassination attempt. The injuries he suffered placed him in a wheelchair. He went in one instant from the highest circles of power to a life-threatening condition.

Displaying a strength of character that few of us will ever know, Jim Brady chose not to ride off into the sunset. He chose not to disappear from view. Instead, he and his wife Sarah chose to bring something good out of this terrible event.

Jim Brady's life had been the American dream come true. He grew up in a small town, got involved in politics, and wound up working with the most powerful man in the free world. He really had it all. But on the day he was shot, as they were taking him to the operating room, a neurosurgeon said, "I don't think he's going to make it." Three television networks took the doctor at his word and prematurely announced that Jim Brady was dead. But like a fighter who refuses to stay down for the count, he defied the odds and made a comeback.

He lived a quality life for three more decades and created a powerful legacy.

The Bradys partnered with an organization called Handgun Control whose watchword is "working to keep handguns out of the wrong hands." Their tireless efforts on behalf of this cause kept Jim Brady in the public eye where he proved every day that where there's a will, there's a way.

As part of the therapy involved in his recovery, Jim Brady had to learn to use parts of his brain that most of us never bother to access. Imagine what the rest of us could do if we would follow his example!

When I asked Jim Brady for his comments for this book, he graciously sent me a copy of *his* book, *Thumbs Up*, and asked his assistant to respond to my questions. His injuries made it difficult for him to express himself as he would have liked. His assistant said:

> *I feel his success in life comes from never giving up and his sense of humor.*

If Jim Brady could fight on and find reasons to laugh, I think we all can. He was fond of saying:

> *When life gives you lemons, you make lemonade. I have several stands around here.*

Jim Brady died more than three decades after the assassination attempt. His death was ruled to be a homicide as it was determined to be a direct result of his gunshot wounds. The assassin's bullet took away the use of his legs and much of his speech, but it never took away Jim Brady's spirit, positive attitude, and lasting legacy.

Brady remained a proponent of responsible gun ownership. In its first year alone, the Brady Law prevented 41,000 convicted felons and other prohibited persons from buying handguns. Jim Brady took the tragedy that occurred on what could have been the worst day of his life and used it to make the world a better place.

ULTIMATE HINDSIGHT

Dave Brubeck

MAKING GOOD (AND ALL THAT JAZZ)

DAVE BRUBECK HAD THE FIRST MILLION-SELLING JAZZ RECORD ever in the United States.

In the music business, it pays to get an early start. Dave Brubeck's mother began teaching him the piano when he was four. He picked up the cello when he was nine, and all those years of training really paid off. By the time he was in his 30s, the jazz quartet that bore his name was a smash hit and remained so for 16 years.

A prolific and original composer, Dave Brubeck is credited with making jazz popular at a time when it wasn't considered "cool." He and his group approached jazz from a different angle and wound up creating a whole new kind of cool.

The comments Mr. Brubeck made to me were brief and had nothing to say about his music career, but it spoke volumes about the way he approached life.

Success and happiness are two very personal conditions defined in a very subjective way. Success is not always measured by recognition or fame nor happiness by material possessions and circumstances.

For me, feeling successful and happy usually derives from the knowledge that my wife and six children are in good health and spiritually thriving. When these basic conditions exist, the secondary desires which affect our lives seem to materialize quite naturally.

But when I or those I love are at risk, a persistent faith that goes beyond human understanding must sustain me. That faith allows me to accept the unexplainable realities of our lives.

When your priorities are in order and your faith is strong, you won't have to go far to find success. It will find you.

Oleg Cassini

A DESIGN FOR SUCCESS

It might appear that Oleg Cassini peaked early. He was, after all, named the principle designer for First Lady Jacqueline Kennedy in 1960. Decades later, however, he was still delighting customers with his unique designs.

Oleg Cassini had his first dress-designing success when he was 13 and living in Italy. He moved to the U.S. in 1936 but had trouble catching on in New York so he moved to Hollywood and began designing costumes for the movie studios. He returned to New York in 1950, became a hit, and never looked back.

Many of the well-known people I've talked with have told me that their "secret" of success is something they read or heard elsewhere. Oleg Cassini was no exception. He found inspiration in the Rudyard Kipling poem "If" and said he especially focused on the line I've highlighted.

For several years, I have given Kipling's famous poem to young people and offered them a cash reward to read the poem and write a report about what it means to them. As a fan of poetry and sometimes-poet myself, I think it may be among the best examples of the genre. Let me share with you part of this great poem.

IF

If you can keep your head when all about you
Are losing theirs and blaming it on you,
If you can trust yourself when all men doubt you,
But make allowance for their doubting, too;
If you can wait and not be tired by waiting,
Or being lied about, don't deal in lies,
Or being hated, don't give way to hating,
And yet don't look too good, nor talk too wise:
If you can dream—and not make dreams your master;
If you can think—and not make thoughts your aim;
If you can meet with Triumph and Disaster
And treat those two imposters just the same...

If you can talk with crowds and keep your virtue,
Or walk with Kings—nor lose the common touch,
If neither foes nor loving friends can hurt you,
If all men count with you, but none too much;
If you can fill the unforgiving minute
With sixty seconds' worth of distance run,
Yours is the Earth and everything that's in it,
And—which is more—you'll be a Man, my son!

Oleg Cassini passed away a few years ago. He is gone but will never be forgotten as long as people look at photos and video from the Camelot era of the Kennedy administration or enjoy great films from the Golden Age of the movie industry.

Joe Castiglione

PLAY BALL, AND WIN AT LIFE

WHEN PEOPLE LEARN THAT I AM A HUGE FAN OF BASEBALL AND rarely miss a game on either broadcast or satellite radio, they often think I'm a fan of sports on the radio because I'm blind. In reality, I became an avid listener of sports broadcast on the radio when I was growing up in the 1960s in Tulsa, Oklahoma, long before I lost my sight. I learned that my little transistor radio that barely picked up Tulsa stations during the day could bring me football, basketball, and baseball games from coast to coast after dark.

I believe the pinnacle of play-by-play radio broadcasting is to become the voice of a major-league baseball team. Listeners come to know these broadcasters throughout the season as if they were an old friend or even a family member.

Joe Castiglione is the voice of the Boston Red Sox. He continues the storied tradition from that historic team. When I asked him to provide his hindsight, he gave me the advice he gives to students and young people today.

> I urge students to follow their dreams and not let anyone discourage them. They truly have to love what they

do but also have to be prepared. Read, read, read on the subject you love. Ask questions and listen. You learn more by listening than by talking. Be open minded with a sense of fairness, and have confidence in your abilities.

Football, basketball, and baseball are just games, but they can teach us a lot about ourselves and a lot about life.

Carol Channing

SAY "HELLO!" TO HARD WORK

CAROL CHANNING HAS WON THREE TONY AWARDS INCLUDING one for Lifetime Achievement, a Golden Globe Award, and has been nominated for an Academy Award.

In 1996, I interviewed Carol Channing during her worldwide tour with *Hello, Dolly!* She has done that role more than 25,000 times, but still brings an energy and an excitement to it that is totally unique in the theatre. She's a perfect example of why I enjoy Broadway theatre both in New York and as presented by the touring companies. I am very proud that here at Narrative Television Network, through FM transmitters, we have opened the world of Broadway theatre to many blind and visually impaired people who otherwise might not have enjoyed this experience.

In all the years I've gone to the theatre, there was only one occasion when the audience gave a standing ovation in the middle of a performance. That was for Carol Channing in *Hello, Dolly!* When I asked her about this during our interview, she told me that it happened every night, and she thought audiences did that for everyone.

What does a performer like Carol Channing have to teach us besides maintaining unbridled enthusiasm? This is what she said to me:

> *Just keep working—keep working wherever you are.*
>
> *I truly live for my work, and I'm fortunate to have a family that understands that. My husband understands it, my son understands it, and the dog understands it. Just live for it.*

Believe me, when you have that sort of attitude about your work, the world will *stand up* and applaud.

Johnnie Cochran, Jr.

BE PREPARED

THERE IS NO DOUBT THAT JOHNNIE COCHRAN WILL ALWAYS BE best remembered as one of the lawyers who helped win an acquittal for O.J. Simpson. After that trial was over, however, he achieved a victory that brought him even more satisfaction. One of his clients, Elmer "Geronimo" Pratt, a man convicted of murder in 1972, was freed in 1997 after it was determined he was wrongly accused. Twenty-five years of effort on Mr. Cochran's part finally paid off.

Johnnie Cochran was busier than ever after the Simpson verdict, writing a book and traveling around the country for speaking engagements until his death in 2005. His first love (next to family), however, was and always remained the law. The key to his success? What he told me was, no doubt, the credo of his law firm.

> *Succinctly put, our three keys to success are **preparation, preparation, preparation**. Always remain focused, and never let anyone deter you from achieving your dreams.*

That's just the kind of summation you would have expected from a lawyer like Johnnie Cochran. Anything worth doing is always worth doing well, and that would include providing justice for all.

ULTIMATE
HINDSIGHT

Ray Conniff

YOU HAVE TO LOVE IT

AT A TIME WHEN ROCK AND ROLL MUSIC WAS MAKING ITS biggest splash, composers like Ray Conniff were producing music that came to be described as "easy listening." He put out a series of successful albums that kept him in the public eye despite the shift to a new and different sound. But Ray Conniff actually began to make his mark long before that time, arranging music for the likes of 1940s "Big Band" leaders Artie Shaw and Harry James.

When a performer becomes a little less visible with the passing of years, you might think that his influence is no longer being felt. That's not the case with Ray Conniff. Let me tell you what he told me:

> *My daughter said the most valuable advice she ever got from me was one day over a double espresso in our kitchen. I told her that she should do what she loves to do the most, and not think about whether she got paid for it or not.*
>
> *That is what I did with my music. I used to write arrangements for bands just to hear them played, and went to sit in at jam sessions evenings in "the Village" of New York City just because I loved to play trombone.*

The result was that I eventually became very successful just doing what I loved to do.

My daughter loves to write, and she is now doing quite well with a new, up-and-coming publishing company in New York City, so I guess it works.

I guess so? No, I *know* so!

Chuck Connors

CONCENTRATE ON THE "FUN"-DAMENTALS

I HAD A CHANCE TO INTERVIEW CHUCK CONNORS SEVERAL YEARS ago, and I can tell you that he truly epitomized the concept of "larger than life." His commanding presence onscreen was not a trick of the cameras.

Few people realize that long before the days of Michael Jordan, Deion Sanders, and Bo Jackson, there was a two-sport athlete named Chuck Connors. He played professional baseball for the Los Angeles Dodgers and basketball for the Boston Celtics. While several athletes in recent times have tried to turn their success on the field or the court into success on the big screen, Chuck Connors never dreamed that baseball would provide the springboard for his jump into acting.

As we talked about how his acting career began, his recollections demonstrated a simple wisdom that I remember to this day.

> I was playing baseball in California. Becoming an actor was the farthest thing from my mind. I had a really good year with the bat and was getting a lot of publicity.
>
> One of the studios called the team and asked about putting me in a small part, and I thought it would be a

59

lot of fun. I was sure they wanted me to play a ball-player. The next day, I showed up at the studio. Not only did they not want me to be a ballplayer, but in my first scene, I was teamed up with Katharine Hepburn and Spencer Tracy!

I remember asking Spencer how you do this, and he said that the key to acting was to "show up on time, know your lines, and hit your mark. And never forget to have fun."

It took me a long time to get the first three, but from the first day on, I have always had fun.

We will always remember Chuck Connors for his starring role on television as *The Rifleman.* Let's also remember what he told us about being punctual, prepared...and having fun.

Bob Costas

BEYOND THE BROADCAST

As a lifelong sports fan and National Champion Olympic Weightlifter myself, Bob Costas first came to my attention—as he did for people around the world—as the host of nine different Olympic games. He has also been a prominent broadcast figure for the NFL, the NBA, and Major League Baseball as well as the US Open Golf Championship.

You can't observe that many top-level performers and champions in action without learning a lot about success. When I asked Bob Costas to draw on his experience and provide some wisdom from his hindsight, he offered the following:

While we all choose our own paths in life, make our own mistakes, and achieve our own successes, one thing I believe is generally true—we do our best and end up happiest when the work we do reflects a genuine interest or passion. Our work is in some way an authentic extension of ourselves; better yet, if that work in some way touches or helps other people. One other thing I have learned along the way is that while high ideals and standards are important, and we can focus so disproportionately on that which is imperfect, we lose sight of much of what is good about ourselves and others. That's about as far as I will go since all of us are, to one extent or another, works in progress. And if we are at all self-aware, there are many times we find ourselves thinking, "If I only knew or understood then, what I know and understand now."

The next time you're tuned in to a baseball, football, or basketball game or even the next Olympics and you hear the familiar voice of Bob Costas, remember what he knows now that he wished he had known back then because you and I know it today.

Bob Cousy

MR. BASKETBALL

BOB COUSY WAS A THREE-TIME ALL AMERICAN IN BASKETBALL AND was drafted third overall in the 1950 NBA draft. He played on six NBA championship teams with the Boston Celtics and was voted onto 13 NBA All-Star teams during his illustrious career which earned him the name Mr. Basketball.

He was 85 years old when I asked him about his view of the world and things he had learned throughout his life and career. While he was cynical regarding some institutions and organizations, he remains positive about people, possibilities, and the human spirit.

At 85 years old, I'm afraid I've lost confidence and respect in many cases for church leaders (Pope Francis excluded—so far), political leaders, business giants (so-called), entertainment greats, etc. It seems to me that once power is achieved, the motto becomes survival and self-interest.

What has sustained my belief and admiration in the human animal has been the sustained and constant achievements of people with disabilities in our world. In every one of life's categories, they use their handicaps as an additional motivator, and for some reason, their successes seem to make them less selfish and more humble and focused.

I applaud you as well. My dear friend and classmate at Holy Cross, Rocks Gallagher, was totally blind and became President of the American Foundation for the Blind. He would travel the world on their behalf (many times without companions).

As someone who has logged over 2 million miles with the airlines, I share Mr. Cousy's respect and admiration for blind people who travel on their own. He reminds us all that it's not as important what we have as what we do with what we have.

His Holiness, The Dalai Lama

DEVELOP YOUR GOOD HUMAN QUALITIES

AS I WAS PULLING TOGETHER THIS BOOK, I STUDIED A NUMBER OF entertainment, business, political, and religious leaders. I have to say that at the beginning I understood very little about the Dalai Lama. I still do not understand a great deal about his faith, but that's not what this book is about.

The Dalai Lama is a Tibetan religious leader. He won the Nobel Peace Prize in 1989 as a result of his appeals for nonviolent liberation of his homeland from Chinese rule. He has been in exile for several decades, but he continues to write and speak about his faith and his search for peace.

When I wrote to the Dalai Lama, I asked him the same question I asked everyone else: What are your thoughts on success and happiness as you look back over your life and career? This is what he shared with me:

> *We have all been born on this earth as part of one great human family. Whatever the superficial differences that distinguish us, each of us is just a human being like everyone else. We all desire happiness and do not want*

65

suffering. What is more, each of us has an equal right to pursue these goals.

Because the very purpose of life is to be happy, it is important to discover what will bring about the greatest degree of happiness. Whether our experience is pleasant or miserable, it is either mental or physical. Generally, it is the mind that exerts the greatest influence on most of us; therefore, we should devote our most serious efforts to bringing about mental peace. In my own limited experience, I have found that the greatest degree of inner tranquility comes from the development of love and compassion....

The more we care for the happiness of others, the greater is our own sense of well-being. Cultivating a close, warm-hearted feeling for others automatically puts the mind at ease. This helps remove whatever fears or insecurities we may have and gives us the strength to cope with any obstacles we encounter. It is the ultimate source of happiness in life.

I believe that at every level of society, from the family up to international relations, the key to a happier and more successful world is the nurturing of compassion. We do not need to become religious, nor do we need to believe in an ideology. All that is necessary is for each of us to develop our good human qualities.

These are words worth pondering regardless of our background, religion, or nationality. Wisdom either works for everyone or it doesn't work for anyone.

Patricia David

WE ALL SUCCEED TOGETHER

PATRICIA DAVID IS THE GLOBAL HEAD OF DIVERSITY FOR JP Morgan Chase. She works in an industry that has not historically been known for its diversity and inclusion. Ms. David is making a difference in her company, her industry, and in the world.

She shared some thoughts with me that can make us all better individually and collectively.

> *Things I wish I'd known when I started my journey:*
>
> *I wish I knew the importance of establishing and building relationships earlier on in my career and that no matter what your job or function is, relationships do matter. I wish I knew that it's important to include others in helping you manage your career, and "don't go it alone." And, lastly, I wish I knew that it's important to follow your own dreams and not try to live in the shadows or follow the dreams of others and the importance of creating your own path to success.*

Either we all succeed together or fail individually. No person is an island.

ULTIMATE
HINDSIGHT

Michael E. DeBakey, M.D.

GETTING TO THE HEART OF SUCCESS

DR. MICHAEL DEBAKEY, WHILE STILL IN MEDICAL SCHOOL AT age 23, helped to develop the roller pump, which 20 years later made heart transplants possible. He received the Presidential Medal of Freedom, the National Medal of Science, and a Congressional Gold Medal. He was cited as a "Living Legend" by the Library of Congress in 2000.

Dr. Michael DeBakey was one of the world's most eminent heart surgeons and the first to complete a successful heart transplant in the U.S. He also pioneered numerous surgical procedures for the treatment of defects and diseases of the circulatory system.

An author and educator whose *firsts* in medicine resulted in lifesaving techniques, Dr. DeBakey proved that if you love and believe in what you are doing, and you aren't afraid to try something new, you can have the kind of success that really means something.

Such a busy person should be hard to reach, but he responded to my letter requesting his thoughts on hindsight less than a week after I mailed it. (Now *that's* the kind of doctor we'd all like to have!) You might think that because of his profession, his chances of succeeding were greater, but as he says here, success is not a profession. It's the way we approach life.

*In my own lexicon, **success** is service to humanity. I was fortunate to have had parents who were models of virtue and to have had a profession that has been intellectually stimulating, psychologically fulfilling, and emotionally gratifying. The result is an exuberance unmatched by any accumulation of wealth, material possessions, or power.*

Real success requires respect for and faithfulness to the highest human values—honesty, integrity, self-discipline, dignity, compassion, humility, courage, personal responsibility, courtesy, and human service. These I learned early from my parents by word and example.

Success is achievable without public recognition, and the world has many unsung heroes. The teacher who inspires you to pursue your education to your ultimate ability is a success. The parents who taught you the noblest human principles are a success. The coach who shows you the importance of team work is a success. The spiritual leader who instills in you spiritual values and faith is a success. The relatives, friends, and neighbors with whom you develop a reciprocal relationship of respect and support—they, too, are successes. The most menial workers can properly consider themselves successful if they perform their best and if the product of their work is of service to humanity.

If, on the other hand, one measures success by public recognition, one may find that it is fleeting, lacking in inner satisfaction and tranquility, and one may then feel disappointment at the fickle finger of fame.

To achieve success, one must have a reasonable, commendable, and achievable goal and must pursue it with determination and dedication. If the goal is humanitarian, the joy will be all the greater.

Dr. Michael DeBakey lived a century here on this earth and focused his professional talents on curing the human heart. His hindsight can help all of our souls, minds, and hearts.

ULTIMATE
HINDSIGHT

Richard M. DeVos

YOU CAN DO IT!

RICHARD DEVOS HAS BEEN RECOGNIZED AS ONE OF THE TEN wealthiest Americans.

Being a platform speaker myself, I always jump at every chance to hear the best speakers in the world. Richard DeVos is among the handful of great motivational speakers of all time.

There are a few people who have revolutionized a product, a company, or even an industry, but Richard DeVos has permanently changed the way that people do business around the world. As the leader of the Amway Corporation, he has a lot to teach us about finding success. This is what he shared with me:

I believe there are three key ingredients in the recipe for success. I call them the "Three As."

The first "A" is "Atmosphere." We need an encouraging atmosphere to achieve our potential. I had very little in the way of material possessions growing up during the Depression, but I was fortunate to have a home with parents who expected me to do my best and work hard to achieve my goals. They never let me get away with saying, "I can't" because they knew I could.

Thanks in large part to my parents, teachers, and other important people in my life who encouraged me, I was able to build a successful business that lets me spend my time encouraging others. When people ask me what I do for a living, I tell them I'm just a cheerleader. I travel around the world doing as my father taught me. To say to people, "You can do it." That's the message people really need to hear to succeed.

The second "A" is "Attitude." We must believe we can reach our goals, and we must be willing to look beyond obstacles to reach them.

Long before my partner, Jay Van Andel, and I started Amway, we dreamed of owning our own business. Our friendship even began with a business arrangement. I paid Jay 25 cents a week for rides to and from school. We knew that when we found the right opportunity, there would be no stopping us from achieving our dream.

The last "A" is "Action." Without action, the other two "As" get us nowhere. We have to jump in and make our dream happen.

It's easy to find reasons not to take action—lack of experience and lack of money are two common excuses. But with the right attitude and atmosphere, we can act despite these roadblocks.

After World War II, Jay and I started our first business—a flying school and our community's first drive-in restaurant. We didn't know anything about either, but we figured that the best way to learn was by doing. We ran these successful businesses for several years before selling them to pursue our next opportunity.

Our next business was selling Nutrilite vitamins person-to-person. We knew nothing about direct selling and even less about vitamins, but we were willing to work hard to learn and to build this business. It was through our experiences with Nutrilite that we developed our plan for Amway.

"Action" also means persevering through setbacks and not giving up just because it would be the easiest thing to do. Jay and I certainly faced our share of problems—like people who thought that "selling soap" would never amount to anything and a fire that destroyed our factory in 1969. It would have been much easier just to let adversity win and get regular jobs like people thought we should. But we never even considered it. And 2.5 million Amway distributors are glad we acted on our dreams instead of our doubts.

I consider myself very blessed to have experienced success. But what is most gratifying about success is the opportunity to help others. When we share our time, money, and experience to help others, we complete the circle of love that leads to our own personal happiness and success.

I have had the privilege on numerous occasions to speak at arena events for the Amway Corporation. On each such occasion as I hear the applause of many thousands of people, I remember that it all began with a dream in the heart, mind, and soul of Rich DeVos.

ULTIMATE HINDSIGHT

Phyllis Diller

Make Up Your Mind

PHYLLIS DILLER, A FUNNY LADY WHO, AT THE HEIGHT OF HER success, probably inspired the term "bad hair day," blazed a trail that female comics have been following ever since. From performing for American soldiers in South Vietnam to her work on stage, television, the radio, as an author, and as a recording artist, she was never afraid to poke fun at herself. As a result, she always gave her audience the gift of laughter.

Do comics have a gene that the rest of us lack? Do they look at the world through Groucho Marx glasses? I wondered what Phyllis Diller would say when I asked her to talk about success.

You ask about success and happiness. Someone said, "You are as happy as you decide to be." I think it was Lincoln or Woody Allen. I don't know.

About success; there are many different ways to measure success. Gandhi only owned one sheet, and he was a success. I know billionaires who are miserable and satiated and don't know a moment of happiness.

It all boils down to spirit and thinking. Everything happens in the mind.

In Phyllis Diller's opinion, you are a success if you think you are a success. You can be happy if you decide to be happy. That means the ball is in *our* court.

Vince Dooley

BULLDOG WITH A HEART

FOR OVER A QUARTER OF A CENTURY, VINCE DOOLEY WAS THE HEAD football coach for the Georgia Bulldogs. He won six Southeast Conference championships during his tenure and one national championship which resulted in him being named Coach of the Year.

Coach Dooley is among the elite in recognizing, recruiting, organizing, and coaching talent. His hindsight has shown him that we all can be judged on our abilities and our performance, not on the things we can't do.

> *As a child growing up in Mobile, Alabama, every person or child with a disability was separated from us in school. I often wondered why but never really asked why.*

> *I grew up in a Catholic school, and we were taught that God created us all in His image, and every person, no matter the color or the disability, was loved and special in His sight.*

> *As I grew older, I had friends with disabilities, both mental and physical, and I realized how important each one was to our world in their own way. Everyone has something to contribute on earth.*

Now I have a grandson with a physical disability (cerebral palsy), and he has taught our family and friends what a positive attitude is and how hard work, trying to stand alone, does pay off. Everyone has goals so don't be afraid to achieve them to the best of your ability.

Remember that God created you just as you are. You are perfect in His sight.

Blessings!

If we are, indeed, perfect in God's sight and Coach Dooley agrees, what else do we need?

Douglas Fairbanks, Jr.

RISE UP

I WILL ALWAYS REMEMBER THE TWO OCCASIONS WHEN I INTERVIEWED Douglas Fairbanks, Jr. No one embodies the classic Hollywood personality more than he does. His father, Douglas Fairbanks, Sr., a standout in silent films, was a megastar in a way that simply does not exist today. Fairbanks, Sr., along with Mary Pickford and Charlie Chaplin, broke the stranglehold that the big studios had on the industry by forming their own studio, United Artists. This legacy of artistic freedom made it possible for Fairbanks, Jr. to blaze his own trail in the business.

Best known for his role in *The Prisoner of Zenda*, Mr. Fairbanks also appeared on stage and in numerous other films in the U.S. and England. He served with the U.S. Navy in World War II, produced more than 160 plays for television, wrote and published his autobiography, *Salad Days*, and took part in several public service missions for the U.S., including a mission to Latin America in the 1940s as a presidential envoy. He grew up surrounded by some of the biggest names in entertainment, business, and politics, and yet he became and remained a gracious and humble man who never lost himself amid the tinsel and footlights.

During one of our interviews, he reflected on his life and expressed satisfaction with his achievements.

At this stage of my life, as I look back on everything that has happened to me, I am most proud of the fact that I created entertainment and an escape for people. This escape allows people to get out of their day-to-day situation and think about the world at large.

Only when we rise above our current circumstance and escape from the day-to-day can we really explore the possibilities.

In speaking about physical conditions (such as blindness) that can create temporary roadblocks on our journey to success, Mr. Fairbanks said:

It is all very well for people who are not blind to preach and lecture in alternative blessing, but I doubt if it is in any way helpful or a consolation. Still, there are many blessings which are available to those with the will and imagination—and the guts—to seek them out, polish them, and then use them as they are intended to be used.

It might be tempting at times to use a physical challenge as an excuse for not succeeding, but it is smarter to go around, over, under, or through the obstacle so that you can take advantage of the good things for you on the other side.

Peter Fonda

A FAMILY DYNASTY OF SUCCESS

IN MOST FAMILIES, IF YOU ARE AN ACADEMY AWARD-NOMINATED movie star, you are a standout—at least among your relatives; but if your father was Henry Fonda, your sister is Jane Fonda, and your daughter is Bridget Fonda, you've got to be at the top of your field just to fit in with your family.

When we made the sequel movie to *The Ultimate Gift* based on my novel *The Ultimate Life*, we were looking for someone to play a Depression-era rancher named Jacob Early who would dispense his wisdom on life and success to a teenager. I was ecstatic when Peter Fonda agreed to play the part. He cared about the message and mission of the film and was great to work with.

I remember during the production I was on a conference call with Peter Fonda and our director Michael Landon, Jr., son of the legendary TV star. Our call was running long, and I was going to have to leave my office in a few moments to attend my father's retirement celebration. They were going to name the theatre at the retirement center, where my father had worked, after my mother and father.

I remember telling Mr. Fonda and Mr. Landon, "Guys, I'm going to have to cut this short. My dad's retiring, and they're dedicating a theatre to him today."

At that point, Peter Fonda stated, "I understand. They named a theatre after my dad in New York."

Michael Landon chimed in, "Yeah, the theatre named after my father is in Los Angeles."

When I arrived at the retirement celebration and stood for a picture with my parents next to the plaque at the theatre entrance which now bears their names, I said, "Today, we join the Fondas and the Landons. It's pretty good company to be in."

Mr. Fonda shared his thoughts on life and success from his own hindsight.

> *I was famous from birth. Getting out from under the shadow of Henry Fonda was difficult. People ask me from time to time what it was like growing up with Henry Fonda as my father. I say, "Ever see Fort Apache? He was like Colonel Thursday."*
>
> *Every director is so different from every other one, and my abilities grow with each job, whether it's writing or directing. I know I'm responsible for not having got the kind of roles that I'd have liked to, but when I stop learning, I'll stop working.*
>
> *I want to die in the saddle. I love writing, producing, acting, directing. I want to be on set and die hearing those words:* **Where's Peter?**

If you get a chance to watch *The Ultimate Life* movie, don't miss Peter Fonda's role as Jacob Early dispensing the same brand of wisdom born from life experience, and if you're ever in Tulsa, Oklahoma, at the University Village Retirement Center, don't miss the George and Florene Stovall Theatre.

ULTIMATE HINDSIGHT

Steve Forbes

MORE THAN MONEY

SEVERAL YEARS AGO, I WAS HONORED TO BE SELECTED BY THE U.S. Chamber of Commerce as the Entrepreneur of the Year. That award brought a lot of recognition and publicity to our great team at the Narrative Television Network and our very special blind and visually impaired audience.

An unexpected benefit that came from that award was my relationship with Steve Forbes. After he heard about the Entrepreneur of the Year award, he contacted me to see if I would be willing to participate with him, Donald Trump, Larry Ellison, Tom Monaghan, and 10 other business leaders in a book entitled *Forbes Great Success Stories*. That book project brought me in regular contact with Steve Forbes, and he has become a colleague, a mentor, and a friend. He wrote the foreword to my book *Ultimate Productivity* and then, several years later, when my novel *The Lamp* was being made into a movie starring Academy Award-winner Louis Gossett, Jr., I asked a few of my business colleagues, including Mr. Forbes, to appear in the movie in a cameo role playing themselves. Steve Forbes was a great sport and did a good job in the movie, but I suggested then and still today that he not give up his day job with *Forbes* magazine to become an actor.

Over the ensuing years, whenever I am in New York City, Mr. Forbes and I carve a few hours out of our schedules and meet in the small private library on the second floor of the Forbes building. We discuss issues of the day, politics, economics, and the important priorities of life.

Following are some of Mr. Forbes' hindsight perspectives on success, happiness, and significance.

What is your purpose? What is your mission? If you have a purpose, everything will come when this purpose is achieved. When you get beyond the bare necessities of life, you begin to do good things for people with your abilities. To be successful and happy you have to meet the needs of other people. We need to make a positive difference in the world through giving, volunteering, being a part of the community.

Everyone has a knack for something, but just because it's tennis, for example, doesn't mean you'll be going to Wimbledon. But if you have a knack for something and a passion, that makes what you do much easier and something you look forward to each day. It gives you a purpose when you do something well. That gives you the intangibles that make life more than just looking for the next weekend.

Someone who loves what they do will probably be thinking about their job or passion all the time and making decisions about how to make it better or provide a more satisfying service. Those small decisions add up over time when you have a real love for what you do and a desire to do it better.

What are the first steps people should take to get from where they are to where they want to be? First, step back and say, "Okay, I have a blank sheet of paper. What could I be doing each day?"

Figure out what you have a passion for and be willing to apply the discipline to achieve that passion. When we go to a sporting event, we see the end result of the game but we don't see all the hard work, sweat, and passion that took place to get the athlete to the event. People who are willing to put in the grunt work and the discipline actually end up being freer than the person who doesn't do anything and ends up unable to do anything at all.

Be prepared for setbacks. Life never goes in a straight line. There will be tradeoffs, but realize it doesn't have to be my way or the highway; and if you don't succeed it doesn't mean you shouldn't try again. You will be a better person, more well-seasoned, more mature, and more prepared to achieve that ultimate goal, even if it isn't in a straight line.

On a daily basis, true happiness to me is getting something done and doing it well whether it's a piece of copy or dealing with a personnel problem; but in a larger sense, you wonder about your own family and their problems. So you worry about a lot of things. There's no such thing as a worry-free life. If you don't have obligations, it means you don't take on responsibilities, so understand that happiness is not just bliss and no worry. It's having the maturity to deal with those in a way so you can get satisfaction in a job well done.

Some people think Steve Forbes shouldn't have any problems, but depending on your religion, the only time you don't worry is when you leave this earth. We all have problems and worries in life that we have no control over, but as Jim Stovall shows us, it's what you do about what's been given you that makes all the difference. Look forward, do what you can with what you have, and amazing things can happen.

Steve Forbes is probably the most-recognized figure in the world relating to money, wealth, and success. He, indeed, has a lot of money, wealth, and success but he has established priorities in his personal and professional life that have made him someone to truly be admired.

Bill Gaither

SONGS AND SUCCESS

I HAVE WRITTEN 30 BOOKS, AND AT THIS WRITING, FOUR OF THEM have been turned into movies. Each time one of these films or books is released, the movie studios or my publishers arrange for me to do a number of interviews. Most of the interviews are done for radio stations or print media and are conducted over the phone, one after the other, so that I might do several dozen interviews in a day. My office staff is very efficient at directing these telephone interviews and letting me know what publication or radio station I am talking to.

One day, I hung up the phone from a radio interview, and Beth, who handles most of our incoming calls, told me, "Bill from *Homecoming* magazine is holding."

I picked up the phone, and the interviewer and I began talking about whatever book or movie project was being released at that time.

As Bill shared a little of his background in asking questions of me, I started to get an inkling that this was someone I should know. When he talked about singing in Las Vegas and meeting Elvis, I blurted out, "You're Bill Gaither." He assured me he was and was a bit surprised that I had not been aware of it.

We have stayed in touch and become friends over the years, and whenever he's in my hometown with one of his touring mega-music concerts in our local arena, we have dinner together backstage before the show.

Bill Gaither's music is about a powerful message. He believes in songs with significance. When I asked him to share his hindsight, looking back over a long and successful career, he stated it succinctly and simply, just as if he were writing one of his song lyrics.

> *It is so easy to let our challenges define us; but I am proof that everyone has something to contribute to this world. Pay attention. Learn from those who have made a difference in the world. Then go out and make a difference with your own unique gifts.*

The next time you hear that Bill Gaither and his traveling band of singers and musicians are going to be in your area, do yourself a favor and spend an evening in their company. Until then, remember his words to live by.

James Garner

A Legend and a Legacy

Growing up in Oklahoma myself, I was always aware of James Garner as he is from my home state. In 2007, Oklahoma celebrated its centennial, and Mr. Garner and I were selected to be in a book entitled *The Top 100 Oklahomans*.

When my first novel, *The Ultimate Gift*, was being made into a movie from 20th Century Fox, I was ecstatic to learn that James Garner would be playing the iconic billionaire in my story, Red Stevens. Red Stevens has been the focal point of four of my books and three movies to date.

I owe a lot to James Garner for believing in me and my message. When he signed on to be a part of *The Ultimate Gift*, the project instantly gained momentum and became a sensation around the world.

Mr. Garner passed away between the time we made the movie and the sequel film, *The Ultimate Life*, but there was enough footage left from the first film's production to include James Garner in the sequel. His role in *The Ultimate Gift* proved to be his last and is ironic as his character Red Stevens has passed away before the movie begins, and he is sharing his wisdom and hindsight with his grandson from beyond the grave. In his thoughts below, Mr. Garner does the same with you and me.

I was a Depression kid growing up in Oklahoma. When I started working, I didn't have a clue what I was doing in that I was just wandering around hoping I could succeed. Then after I got a little under my belt, it took me about 25 years to feel like I knew what I was doing. I've had to work very hard at that easy-going manner you see on the screen.

Everybody wants blockbusters. I like to see a few pictures now and then that have to do with people and have relationships, and that's what I want to do films about. I don't want to see these sci-fi movies, and I don't want to do one of those. I don't understand it. The characters I've played, especially Bret Maverick and Jim Rockford, almost never use a gun, and they always try to use their wits instead of their fists.

I don't take success very well because I know it's fleeting. And the next day, it can all fall apart. I know that, too. So I don't get too high, and I don't get too low. You get through the world a lot easier that way. My goal has always been longevity, not fame and fortune. Just get a job, and keep it.

James Garner was a great talent and a great man who used his influence to create a message and leave a legacy.

Jerry Glanville

POINTS TO PONDER

JERRY GLANVILLE WAS A SUCCESSFUL FOOTBALL PLAYER BUT BEST known as a coach for the NFL Houston Oilers and Atlanta Falcons. Later, he became a highly-sought-after analyst for network television football broadcasts. He has the distinction of coining the phrase: "NFL stands for *Not For Long*." Though he was criticizing a referee at the time, the phrase *Not For Long* has been adopted by many pro football players to express their thoughts about how short an athletic career can be and that one should enjoy every moment of every day.

When I asked Coach Glanville to share his own hindsight thoughts of things he knows now he wished he had known before, he drew on his coaching experience to condense his message into six brief points.

1. *Be positive about all opportunities.*

2. *Never take credit.*

3. *Discouragement cannot enter.*

4. *Enjoy the moment.*

5. *False praise cheapens real praise.*

6. *Work harder than everyone that works with you.*

Coach Glanville reminds us all that time is fleeting, and this life is *Not For Long*; therefore, we need to apply his six success principles and get the most out of every moment.

Louis Gossett, Jr.

MORE THAN AN OFFICER AND A GENTLEMAN

I HAD THE PRIVILEGE OF MEETING AND WORKING WITH LOUIS Gossett, Jr. when my book *The Lamp* was turned into a movie. Writing lines for an Academy Award-winning actor like Louis Gossett, Jr. is a great thrill, privilege, and responsibility. Mr. Gossett was everything I hoped he would be and more. He embodied the message of *The Lamp* movie and was kind and gracious to all of us who worked with him on the set.

Louis Gossett, Jr. has enjoyed an incredible movie career, and long after most people have retired, he is still busy making films. At this stage in his career, he told me he is most interested in movie parts that help him express his faith and his philosophies on living a successful life.

When I asked him to share his hindsight thoughts, he spoke candidly and directly.

The worst resentment that anybody can have is one you feel justified to keep. I am dedicating the last of my life to an all-out conscientious offensive against racism. Violence is a war, and I would pray that the energy we exert on war gets reverted back to a communal effort to save the planet. So perhaps in my own small way I can generate some energy toward the salvation of the planet because when we win a war, we win a dying planet.

I think what's more important than law is the hearts of the people. We need to do whatever it takes to get our children together and pay attention to them because that's our future. What's in the hearts and minds of our children is what's in our future.

We all have a bout with death and things that touch our mortality. When that happens, all that bling-bling gets thrown away because all you've got is you and God. The Lord may not come when you want Him, but he's always going to be there on time. I'm cancer-free. I'm on antioxidants and acupuncture and a different diet, and I have a different outlook on life. I don't have resentment any more. It's wonderful.

Louis Gossett has become a good friend and mentor to me. He has often shared with me stories about being raised by his great grandmother who was born a slave. He has seen hatred and love as well as failure and success, and through it all, Lou Gossett has been the soul of grace and dignity, which has made him a star on the big screen and a true success in life.

Peter Graves

SUCCESS IS *MISSION: POSSIBLE*

I MET PETER GRAVES WHEN I INTERVIEWED HIM FOR MY NARRATIVE Television Network *NTN Showcase* program. Mr. Graves is probably best known for his lead role on the hit TV show *Mission: Impossible* as well as being the host of the nightly *Biography* show on A&E. A generation of young people became familiar with Peter Graves through his satirical comedy roles in the *Airplane* movies.

Mr. Graves came to Hollywood following in the footsteps of his older brother, James Arness, star of the long-running TV series *Gunsmoke* where he played the iconic figure Matt Dillon. Peter Graves learned from his brother but built his own career in which he didn't have to stand in anyone's shadow.

He had some great thoughts to share about wisdom he gained throughout his life and career.

> *I guess success in life means many different things to many different people, but it certainly was most important to me that I had a goal that I had my eye on.*
>
> *That goal was "something I must do," and I persevered until I got it done or got a start at it. Then you stay on top of it, and keep punching and pushing and striving all*

99

the time to go in the directions that you want, whatever it is in life that you want.

Generations of people who enjoyed Peter Graves' work on the big screen and through his television programs saw him as a calm, cool, and collected character. They never saw the persistence and hard work behind the scenes that made him a star in his career and a success in his life.

Don Green

THINK, GROW RICH, AND PASS IT ON

ON GREEN HAD A SUCCESSFUL CAREER AS A BANKER, AND AT AN age when most people are looking to retire, Don accepted a position as the Executive Director of The Napoleon Hill Foundation.

I met Don through an appearance he made on TV with Oprah. We became friends, and he has given me the opportunity to work on several projects in conjunction with The Napoleon Hill Foundation. He is a true friend and mentor and dedicates his life to keeping the mission and message of Napoleon Hill alive and growing.

His hindsight thoughts are instructive to us all.

> *One of the things I wish I had learned earlier in my life was to appreciate my parents more than I did. Both were young people during the Depression, and the adversities they faced were overcome by faith and hard work. Like most parents, they wanted their children to have a good life.*

Sometimes we do not realize what a blessing it is to have parents with such outstanding traits until we start a family of our own.

As a young person, I compared material items that I did not have with others who had more. Life became easier once I learned to count my blessings. I began to realize I had more than most and was in an excellent position in life to have a positive impact on others, especially young people with whom our future rests. They are a true gift from God.

Don Green is committed to helping others succeed. He has given 21st century authors like me the privilege of collaborating on books, audios, and DVD projects with the monumental Napoleon Hill. Don always seems to find a way to give others the limelight which, in the long run, is the seed of his own success and legacy.

Alexander Haig

DO YOUR LEVEL BEST

IN THE U.S., YOU DON'T GET MUCH MORE SUCCESSFUL THAN BEING named Secretary of State. And you don't get chosen for that post unless you have outstanding credentials and experience.

Alexander Haig more than met the requirements of the job. He was, after all, a graduate of the U.S. Military Academy, the Naval War College, and the Army War College. He became a general in 1973, was chief of staff at the White House, and served as commander-in-chief of the U.S. European Command. He was definitely someone you want to talk to when you are writing a book on success.

In responding to my request for his comments, this is what he said:

> *Whatever you do, make a difference.*
>
> *Practice rather than preach. Be a realist but only to change the world guided by your principles. There is justice though often well-disguised. Make of your life an affirmation, defined by your ideals, not the negation of others. Dare to the level of your capability, then go beyond to a higher level.*
>
> *If you would be fit to command men, obey God.*

I might add, if you can't be a leader, be the best follower you can possibly be. When you do your best, you are a success.

Monty Hall

MAKE A DEAL AND SLEEP WELL

ON A TELEVISION GAME SHOW, WHO REALLY WINS? IS IT THE contestant who receives the new car, the $25,000, and the vacation of a lifetime? Is it the members of the audience who share in the excitement of the moment? Is it the members of the crew for whom the show provides steady employment? Or perhaps it's the show's creator who earns a small fortune from syndication rights.

Yes, all those people derive some degree of happiness from a game show. But in the case of Monty Hall, host of the long-running (22 years!) *Let's Make a Deal*, it was the emcee who walked away a winner.

In the midst of, and especially after, a successful show like *Let's Make a Deal*, you could understand it if the star decided to simply do his job and be a good citizen. But Monty Hall wouldn't rest until he shared his bounty with others. Are you looking for happiness? Read this, and learn.

> *When I was a youngster, I never thought I would grow out of the poverty of my surroundings. Fate was kind to me, and I managed to achieve more than I ever dreamed*

of. Thus, I can honestly say I never was hungry for even greater success.

My television success brought me fame and financial rewards. But it is the way I used these that is the real secret of my happiness. I have a great marriage, wonderful children and grandchildren, and have devoted my life to helping others. I spend 200 days a year traveling, speaking, and raising money for countless charities.

There is a saying, "It is better to give than to receive." I place my own creed next to that. "There are givers and takers in the world. The takers eat well; the givers sleep well."

I sleep well.

Mark Victor Hansen

CHICKEN SOUP FOR THE WORLD

MARK VICTOR HANSEN HAS SOLD MORE BOOKS THAN ANY other living author. His *Chicken Soup for the Soul* series literally revolutionized the publishing industry. I met Mark when he agreed to write an endorsement for my book *The Ultimate Gift*. He revolutionized my career and my life when he said, "I see *The Ultimate Gift* as one of the greatest motion pictures of all time."

That novel sold millions of copies, and I believe Mark's words planted the seeds in the minds of the executives at 20th Century Fox that eventually brought that story and sequels of *The Ultimate Gift* to the big screen.

Mark, who could have retired and lived lavishly off his royalties many years ago, works harder than ever to share his message of hope and possibility. He wanted me to share the following with you.

Each of us has some inherent limitations, disabilities, or unique challenges, whether or not we are sighted or unsighted. We must create our own magnificent obsession that will be our dream come true.

The critical desire is to control our thinking, feeling nature and attitudes. Sometimes it feels that each of us is being unfairly treated. Assuming we choose to stay positive, find solutions, overcome adversities, and be self-determining in our attitudes, we can individually and collectively reach ever-higher altitudes of success, abundance, and relationship bliss.

Mark Victor Hansen is one of those people who makes the world a better place by helping each individual change their own world. His words can impact you and the people you come in contact with every day.

Paul Harvey

GOOD DAY!

I WAS BORN AND RAISED IN TULSA, OKLAHOMA, WHERE I MAKE MY home to this day. The most famous Tulsan of all time may well have been Paul Harvey. He began working on the air at a local radio station when he was still in high school. His talent and tenacity soon put him on the national and the world stage.

For several generations of people, Paul Harvey *News and Comment* was a daily fixture. People gathered around radios each morning and midday to hear the news delivered to them as if Paul Harvey were their neighbor talking across the back fence. His "rest of the story" broadcasts let people look behind the façade of the people, places, and events they thought they knew to learn the deeper truths beyond.

I met Paul Harvey when he called my office after reading one of my books. When my phone buzzed, and they told me that Paul Harvey was calling, I thought, *It's a common name*, but I asked, "Is it *the* Paul Harvey?"

The immediate response was, "I don't think anyone else can talk like that."

Paul Harvey endorsed several of my books and became a mentor and friend. He was one of the best speakers I ever heard. Whether he was speaking from the stage or his radio microphone,

Mr. Harvey made everyone feel as if he were speaking directly to them.

He never took his mission or his message for granted. Every time he broadcast the news, he did so standing at a podium wearing a suit and tie. He told me, "Whether I'm going to church, out on the town with my beloved bride Angel, or talking to my friends on the radio, I believe in dressing like it matters...because it does."

Mr. Harvey wrote much of the news copy he read to us on the radio for years. He had the unique talent of capturing complex thoughts and emotions in a brief phrase. Here's Mr. Harvey's hindsight in headline form.

> *In times like these, it helps to recall that there have always been times like these.*
>
> *Like what you do. If you don't like it, do something else.*
>
> *When your outgo exceeds your income, the upshot may be your downfall.*
>
> *Every pessimist who ever lived has been buried in an unmarked grave. Tomorrow has always been better than today, and it always will be.*
>
> *I've never seen a monument erected to a pessimist.*
>
> *Retiring is just practicing up to be dead. That doesn't take any practice.*

Paul Harvey became famous for his signature signoff at the end of each broadcast. He would finish a news story and then announce, "Paul Harvey," followed by a long pause and then end his broadcast with the simple admonition, "Good day."

He told me as a rookie broadcaster, his manager's only advice before his first-ever live newscast was to simply read the script exactly and finish precisely at the top of the hour. Apparently, Mr. Harvey had several seconds left over at the end of that inaugural broadcast and just remained silent 'til the top of the hour, leaving what he liked to call his "pregnant pause."

The last time I ever spoke to him on the phone, he left me with the words he left the world with throughout his life. "Good day!"

ULTIMATE
HINDSIGHT

Helen Hayes

SET THE STAGE

ELEN HAYES WAS BORN IN 1900, AND HER SHOW BUSINESS career spanned most of the 20th century. Among her many awards, she received a Tony, an Emmy, a Grammy, and multiple Oscars. She was awarded the Presidential Medal of Freedom for her contribution to the performing arts.

I was privileged to interview Helen Hayes, the First Lady of the American Stage, late in her life. I see her as an actress who bridged the worlds of movies and theatre better than anyone before or since.

During each of my celebrity interviews, I ask movie stars about other people they have worked with. Not all of the comments are positive, but I have never heard anyone say anything but the very best about Helen Hayes.

I asked her what she wanted to be remembered for.

I will be remembered however I am remembered. I have no control over that.

The things I value are the efforts I have made on behalf of my craft and the theatre, in general, that no one will ever know about.

I have attempted to be a great force for the stage and theatre as a whole.

It was important for Helen Hayes, and it is important for us to see our work as something that will result in an outcome larger than our own individual contribution. To realize a meaningful success, we need to work for "the greater good" and not for a flowery eulogy.

Katharine Hepburn

PURSUE YOUR PASSION

WHEN I LOOK BACK OVER MY 30-YEAR BUSINESS CAREER TO date, I have had a number of big breaks. One of the biggest was to get to meet and work with Katharine Hepburn.

Narrating movies and TV shows to make them accessible for blind and visually impaired people was all we had in mind when we created the Narrative Television Network. There was no thought of doing celebrity interviews for the talk show.

In 1989, we got a huge break and were able to launch our network with several hundred affiliates across the country. As part of the deal, I agreed to deliver two-hour blocks of programming at various times of the day and night throughout the week. The problem was, our movies did not fit that time schedule, so we were faced with dead air time on national television. To fill this dead time, my immediate thought was to conduct interviews with the movie stars who appeared in the movies we were showing.

And so, we went to the library and found a book entitled *Addresses of the Stars*. We mailed letters to some of the biggest names in show business asking them to be a part of this new network. The first positive response I received was from Katharine Hepburn. I knew this was big, but I didn't know *how* big. You see, every celebrity who called to inquire about the show would ask what other guests had already been on. Being able to tell them that Katharine Hepburn had been on the show opened every door.

Between 1933 and 1981, Miss Hepburn won four Oscars and received eight additional Academy Award nominations for her work. *The Philadelphia Story, Guess Who's Coming to Dinner,* and *The African Queen* are three of her most memorable films. Someone as celebrated as she should have been used to the interview process, but Miss Hepburn was a very private person to whom interviews did not come easily. For this reason, I will always be grateful to her for sitting down and talking with me.

I remember asking her about her career and what she might have done had she not been an actress.

I am thankful that I can make a living as an actress. If I could not, I would have to find another way to support myself as I pursue my passion.

Katharine Hepburn taught me then that nothing succeeds bigger or better than a driving passion for your life's work. All of us need to find that passion in our work or find work where we can experience the passion.

Most jobs don't come with annual awards ceremonies, but we can feel like winners as long as we do what we absolutely love.

Charlton Heston

SPEND TIME WISELY

CHARLTON HESTON WAS AN ACADEMY AWARD-WINNING ACTOR and one of the last superstars from the Golden Age of the movie industry. He was always mindful of his presence on and off the screen. In 2003, suffering from Alzheimer's, he felt he could no longer present the persona he wanted to, so he made a conscious decision to end his public life. For the remaining five years of his life, he was devoted to friends and family.

When we first started the Narrative Television Network and the very special work we do, we were struggling for credibility in the broadcast, cable, and entertainment industries. There were several people who took the time and effort to write us a letter of support and encouragement. One of the first letters we received was from Charlton Heston. It meant everything to us then, and it still does today. That letter is displayed in our office.

Charlton Heston has played roles such as Moses and Ben Hur that will forever make him seem larger than life. The reality is, he had a life larger than that of the ordinary person, but his message to us is that we *all* can live larger than life.

One of the most powerful lessons that Charlton Heston taught us is not about stardom or career but about personal and family life:

The best thing my wife, Lydia, and I gave our children was our time, which we did not so much out of a feeling that we must ("quality time"…what an ugly phrase), but because we liked it.

Love is, or should be, a given.

*I **liked** driving (my daughter) Holly to ballet lessons or lip-syncing show tunes with her to records while she cavorted in makeshift costumes, just as Lydia liked teaching both kids to swim, and we both loved reading to them.*

In his autobiography, *In the Arena*, Charlton Heston said that in looking back there was nothing he would want to change, that life had been *too good* to him. Perhaps that is because with all his success in the world of entertainment, the world he created with his family managed to stay center stage.

Lou Holtz

GO WITH WHAT YOU KNOW

FOOTBALL COACH LOU HOLTZ LED NOTRE DAME TO THE NATIONAL championship in 1988 in just his third year on the job. In 1988-89, his team also achieved its longest consecutive winning streak—23 games.

The job of head football coach at Notre Dame is considered by many to be the best coaching job in the nation. It was a job that Lou Holtz had earned. He began his coaching career in the late 1950s while he was working on his bachelor's degree. He went on to coach at several other colleges and universities and, at one point, with the New York Jets.

When he was named National Coach of the Year in 1988, Lou Holtz appeared to have reached the pinnacle of success. When he lost his job nearly a decade later, it looked like the end of a dream. As it happened, I had written to ask him for his comments on success at precisely the time his tenure at Notre Dame was coming to an end. What he had to say to me at that difficult time was:

> *I feel blessed to have had the opportunity to coach at the University of Notre Dame. I do not know what the future holds, but I do know who holds the future.*

119

You get the impression that no matter where Lou Holtz finds himself, his outlook on life is going to see him through every time.

Lee Iacocca

DRIVEN TOWARD SUCCESS

LEE IACOCCA HAS BEEN VOTED AMONG THE TOP 20 BUSINESS executives of all time. He has the distinction of developing the Ford Mustang and the Chrysler minivan. Both vehicles permanently altered the industry.

You will see in his comments below he has a true passion for automobiles and the business arena.

> Your letter arrived at a most opportune moment since someone walked into my home and the subject was about the passion in what a person chooses to do with their life. This is a good place to start. I believe if a person follows their passion, they will ultimately be a success. And sticking to a career path is a good way to achieve this.
>
> In my autobiography, I write, "When the chips were down, my mother found nothing wrong with working in the silk mills so I could have lunch money for school. She did what she had to do. When I got to Chrysler, I found a royal mess, but I did what I had to do." What we can take from this is no job is too menial, and all work has value. Sometimes a person needs to make difficult decisions for the greater good.

*Giving back, no matter what a person's personal circumstances, is one of the best ways to reap the rewards of living in this wonderful country. I say in my book **Where Have All The Leaders Gone?**, "Each of us has to put something back in. Let's start a dialogue about public service. The point is very simple: There is no free lunch. For everything you get, you have to give something back."*

These two principles are so important to have a good life, and I have tried to live my life by an ethical code of conduct.

I will always remember Lee Iacocca's concept that integrity reigns, and it is more important how we succeed than how much we succeed.

Billy Joel

THE PIANO MAN

BILLY JOEL HAS SOLD OVER 100 MILLION ALBUMS, MAKING HIM one of the bestselling recording artists of all time, and he has been inducted into the Rock and Roll Hall of Fame. The Broadway show entitled *Movin' Out* is based on Billy Joel's songs and his career.

As a musician, he creates the mood, but as a writer, he creates a message. You will discover some of his wit and wisdom in his comments below.

> *I think music, in itself, is healing. It's an explosive expression of humanity. It's something we are all touched by. No matter what culture we're from, everyone loves music. I wish I were less of a thinking man and more of a fool not afraid of rejection.*
>
> *Musicians want to be the loud voice for so many quiet hearts. If you make music for the human needs you have within yourself, then you do it for all humans who need the same things. You enrich humanity with the profound expression of these feelings. As human beings, we need to know that we are not alone, that we are not crazy or completely out of our minds, that there are*

other people out there who feel as we do, live as we do, love as we do, who are like us.

You're not the only one who has made mistakes, but they are the only things that you can truly call your own. I am no longer afraid of becoming lost, because the journey back always reveals something new, and that is ultimately good for the artist. Don't make music for some vast, unseen audience or market or ratings share or even for something as tangible as money. Though it's crucial to make a living, that shouldn't be your inspiration. Do it for yourself.

The good ole days weren't always good, and tomorrow ain't as bad as it seems.

As someone who plays at playing the piano myself, I'm just good enough to respect someone like Billy Joel; however, when I think about his statement, "I wish I were less of a thinking man and more of a fool not afraid of rejection," I realize that's the difference between playing at life and living it well.

Charlie "Tremendous" Jones

A Man Called "Tremendous"

Charlie "Tremendous" Jones was a legend in the personal development field. In the 1960s, he produced an audio series and a book entitled *Life Is Tremendous*. From that time until his death, he was known around the world as Charlie "Tremendous" Jones. Later in his career, he founded his own publishing company known as Executive Books, and it continues today as Tremendous Life Books.

I have written 30 books to date with more than 10 million copies in print in over two dozen languages. By far the biggest break I ever got in the publishing world was when Charlie Jones agreed to publish my first little novel entitled *The Ultimate Gift*. I had written seven nonfiction books before that, but none of my publishers nor anyone else in the publishing industry seemed to believe that Jim Stovall could be a novelist.

Charlie read the book and called me from an airport, exclaiming, "This is the best book I've read in 20 years!" That statement meant a lot coming from Charlie Jones because he was a voracious reader and may have done more to encourage reading around the world than anyone else of his era.

Not only did Charlie publish *The Ultimate Gift*, but he insisted on giving me a release clause from the contract "once a major publisher wants the title." That day came, but I insisted that the major publishing group allow Charlie "Tremendous" Jones to continue publishing his own version of *The Ultimate Gift* in perpetuity.

Charlie "Tremendous" Jones had a deep wisdom and a compelling enthusiasm that impacted everyone he met. I believe his words can impact you now.

> *Everyone has a success mechanism and a failure mechanism. The failure mechanism goes off by itself. The success mechanism only goes off with a goal. Every time we write down and talk about a goal, we push the button to start the success mechanism.*
>
> *No one is a failure until they blame somebody else.*
>
> *Things don't go wrong and break your heart so you can become bitter and give up. They happen to break you down and build you back up so you can be all that you were intended to be.*
>
> *Leaders are readers.*
>
> *You will be the same person in five years as you are today except for the people you meet and the books you read.*

I became a better writer, a better businessperson, and a better man because I knew Charlie "Tremendous" Jones. When you read any of my novels or watch the movies based on them, remember they would have never been possible without the belief of one tremendous individual—Charlie "Tremendous" Jones.

Shirley Jones

WRITE YOUR OWN RULES

WHEN WE TALK ABOUT SUCCESS, WE SOMETIMES FORGET THAT it isn't just about our careers. It's also about our families. So I'm glad that when Shirley Jones answered my request for her thoughts on success, she chose to send me something she wrote that has to do with making a success of marriage.

She could have talked about landing the lead role of Laurey in her first movie, the musical *Oklahoma!*, or winning the Academy Award for *Elmer Gantry*, or being one of America's favorite moms on the television series *The Partridge Family*. Instead, she sent me the script of an anniversary card she created for her husband on their tenth anniversary. Called "The Ten-Word Manual for Marriage," it has some tips that also apply to getting along with people you *aren't* married to. (Let's face it: If you know how to get along with people, you are a lot more likely to succeed in *all* areas of your life.)

I want to share just a few of Shirley Jones's *Ten Words* with you.

Truth. The only way to go, with anything, especially love. And there is absolutely no defense against it; it is the purest communication there is. Try it, with yourself first…. Work on it. It will lift all the weight off your shoulders.

Humor. *Easier said than done, but do it, find it, feel it, look for partners with it. Life's absurd as it is. Try laughing at it. Just make the* **sound** *first. It's contagious and medicinal and addictive.*

Self-Esteem. *The magic words. If you won't muster any for you, nobody else will…. Any spare time, work on liking yourself better. It'll put a new paint job on everything.*

Change. *There's always someone to tell you that you have to.* **Wrong. Don't.** *Rather, spend time finding out who you* **really** *are. Work on being more of* **that**. *A lot better than the futile "gotta change" treadmill, which never really ends.*

There are lots of books (with lots of lists) that presume to tell you how to live your life. My advice: Pull out only the concepts that you believe will work for you and then make your own list. As Shirley Jones has shown us, we can look at who and where we are, decide what and where we want to be, and come up with our own plan for getting the most out of our lives. It won't be easy, but it will definitely be worth the effort.

Joye Kanelakos

THE HEART OF A POET

EACH OF MY 30 BOOKS (INCLUDING THE ONE YOU'RE READING right now), my approximately 1,000 syndicated newspaper columns, and my screenplays for movies have all been typed and edited by a talented colleague named Dorothy Thompson. Several years ago, we were working on one of my writing projects when Dorothy got the call telling her that her mother had a stroke, and Dorothy should come home as soon as possible to Kansas where her mother lived.

Dorothy got to spend some priceless time with her mother before she passed. During those conversations, her mother told her about a box on the top shelf of the closet that she should take a look at. After Dorothy's mother's funeral, Dorothy and her sister opened the box and discovered that it was filled with poetry that her mother had written throughout her life.

I asked Dorothy to share some of the poetry with me, and I was so impressed that I wrote a book called *Discovering Joye* which contained dozens of Joye Kanelakos's poems along with my own commentary.

When I considered hindsight, looking back on a life well-lived, I wanted to share Joye Kanelakos's message and gift with you.

I awoke this morning
With a prayer of gratefulness,
A prayer of hopefulness,
And joy.
To a God of love, I asked for love—
A house filled with it.
I seek and expect a home
Bursting its seams
And raising the roof
With love.
Driving out everything else
And making a place for angels to enter
And sing of the promise,
"Where love is,
There I am, also."

This poem and all of Joye's poetry offers a new vision of the world around us and the possibilities in our lives. I hope you will capture a new vision of who you can become and what gifts lie hidden inside of you.

The Amazing Kreskin

STOP AND LISTEN

THE AMAZING KRESKIN HAS APPEARED ON HIS OWN TV SHOW AND in countless performances around the world for more than 50 years. As a mentalist, he is one who perceives and reads other people's thoughts. Although most would consider this a gift, Kreskin believes it is an ability that, to a certain degree, can be developed.

In his letter to me, he said that oftentimes when a person loses his eyesight late in life his hearing becomes more acute. He hears someone approaching from a distance long before the sighted person who is with him is aware of it. And in some cases, he knows *who* is approaching before he receives any aural cues.

What does this have to do with success? It tells us that if we have a weakness in one area, we can develop a strength in another in order to compensate. It also tells us that we need to listen if we are going to get the information we need to come to a correct conclusion or come up with a sensible solution.

Kreskin said, "Orson Welles once said to me, 'The worst thing that happened to movies was color.' It was too distracting. Motion and action that attracts the eye can often detract from our inner sensitivity to what is being said or done before us." In other words, we put so much emphasis on what we see that we get lazy in our efforts to listen to and interpret the meaning of what is being said.

Kreskin said he looks upon his work as an adventure and himself as "an adventurer exploring probably the greatest riddle of all: the human mind." He gave this advice:

> To those who do not exhibit my abilities as a thought reader, I might give my strongest advice, and that is to listen and listen fully before responding or commenting on something that is said or mentioned in a conversation. Pause and listen.
>
> Too many people are afraid of silence. It is as if something has to be happening all the time. But often, with silence, there is more happening. There is a reflection on what was really said to us, what was really meant by the remarks, and, yes, perhaps some passage of thought between that person and ourselves.

You don't have to have ESP to get ahead, but you do need to *pay attention.*

John Kundla

A HALL OF FAME LIFE

JOHN KUNDLA IS THE OLDEST LIVING HALL OF FAMER IN ANY MAJOR sport. In his 98th year, his competitive energies are focused more on bingo at the Main Street Lodge Assisted Living Center than being a Hall of Fame NBA player or coaching his pro teams to nine championships.

For many years, my father ran a retirement center and nursing home. I came in contact with many people in their 80s, 90s, and even those over 100 years. I have come to the conclusion that we all want to have many years of life, but it may be more important in hindsight to look at how much life we had in our years.

John Kundla expresses a joy and enthusiasm for the life he has today and is still looking forward.

> *Celebrating my 98th birthday. I was born July 3, 1916. I attribute this to being a gym teacher. I received a physical education degree at the University of Minnesota in 1939. I played basketball and baseball in high school and college to stay in good condition. To this day, I have a stationary bike to stay in shape.*
>
> *I'm proud of my grandchildren. All of them are A students, and all of them have scholarships to college. Their*

parents were both high school teachers. Three of the family have college degrees, and three are in college now.

As a student of human beings, I have come to the conclusion that we live well as long as we assume our best days are ahead. I'm reminded of the famous quote from Satchel Paige: "Don't look back. Something might be gaining on you."

The best is yet to come.

Dorothy Lamour

HAVE A SENSE OF HUMOR

DOROTHY LAMOUR WILL ALWAYS BE REMEMBERED FOR HER ROLES in the *Road* shows, a series of movies she did with Bob Hope and Bing Crosby. She also had the good fortune of being considered one of the most beautiful women of her time. (Put a "G" in front of her last name, and you'll get the picture.)

When I interviewed her, she had a great perspective on the way Hollywood sometimes works. She realized that her looks got her into the movies, but that her talent kept her working; and she was very pleased that beyond her devastating beauty, she simply brought people joy. She said to me:

> *As I look back, I am most proud that I made people laugh. The world takes itself far too seriously; laughter is something there's far too little of. Whatever one does, they should always remember to laugh.*

Dorothy Lamour was right. Not everything that happens to us—and certainly not every decision we make—is a matter of life and death. We need to lighten up a little, look on the bright side a little more often, and remember that it takes more muscles to frown than it does to smile.

If we can bring laughter into someone else's life, we will have achieved a very special kind of success.

Janet Leigh

MAKE THE WORLD BETTER

SAY *JANET LEIGH* AND WHAT COMES TO MIND IS LIKELY HER chilling shower scene in *Psycho*. But her fans also loved her in the musical comedy *Bye Bye Birdie* as well as in dozens of other films.

When I asked her to tell me what success and happiness meant to her, she shared with me a wonderful story about someone very near and dear to her. I think you will find it inspiring.

*My grandmother was blind, and it—**it** being the word and the condition—didn't mean much to me as a child. This was just the way she was, and she didn't seem so different from the rest of the family. She cooked, she ironed, she did the laundry, she chopped kindling, she played the piano.*

And then one day, after I found out what blind meant, I made believe I couldn't see. I shut my eyes tightly and attempted to do what I normally did. But I couldn't do anything. I became so frantic and quickly opened my eyes so I could be safe again.

But Grandma couldn't see even when she opened her eyes; she wasn't playing a game. It was at that time I realized what a great woman she was and how courageously she had met and overcome a tremendous challenge. I never heard her complain, or say, "Why me?" She was almost always smiling, caring, interested, and interesting.

She taught me the greatest lesson in living that I could ever learn. Any time I would feel blue, or unlucky, or deprived, or jealous, or anything negative, I would think of her and understand how blessed I was.

She made the world better because she was in it.

My grandmother made me want to leave the world a better place than when I came into it—just like she had.

When I heard that Janet Leigh had died in 2004, I remember thinking of the story she shared about her grandmother. As a blind person myself, it always meant a lot that she had shared that story with me.

When my novels started being turned into movies, I got very involved in the process of taking stories from the page and putting them on the screen. Movies are an impactful medium. This is supported by the fact that most film critics agree that the most terrifying scene ever filmed was the one Janet Leigh did for the Hitchcock film *Psycho*. If you have a chance to rent or stream that movie sometime, watch the shower scene and realize you really don't see anything at all. The fear and terror are in your mind.

That's an important lesson for us all to learn and a great legacy that Janet Leigh leaves behind.

Jack Lemmon

ROLL WITH THE PUNCHES

JACK LEMMON WAS A TWO-TIME ACADEMY AWARD WINNER, AND ONE of my earlier interviews on NTN was with Mr. Lemmon. Since that time, I have written plays and actually performed in a brief play in a show we produced called *Discover Your Destiny*. *Discover Your Destiny* is designed to create a complete theatre experience by taking my platform-speaking information and putting it together with celebrities on the big screen, music, lights, and drama. That brief play was eventually expanded into my novel *The Lamp* that was later turned into a major motion picture starring Academy Award winner Louis Gossett, Jr.

I probably owe my exploration of playwriting and acting to Jack Lemmon more than to anyone else. He brought an energy and a passion to every role that few actors have ever managed to duplicate.

This Oscar-winning, Emmy-winning Harvard graduate was one of those rare actors who could do comedy as effortlessly as he did drama. He first appeared on Broadway at the age of twenty-eight. Soon after, he made his way to television and then began the film career that made him a fixture on the big screen for more than 40 years.

Many of Jack Lemmon's films had to do with the issues of the day. *The China Syndrome* concerned the potential dangers of nuclear power plants. As you read what he had to say to me on the subject of success, I think you will agree that this enduring entertainer was a man who took very seriously the impact he had on his audience.

> *When I think about the accomplishments of my career, I do not look at the individual highs and lows but at the overall body of work.*
>
> *We don't live and die on one success or failure.*
>
> *I am pleased that my career has brought laughter and entertainment to people, but I consider it a rare privilege that I have caused people from time to time to stop and think about who they are and how they stand on important issues in their lives and in the world.*

Achieving success can be thrilling, but it is a lot more satisfying if you can make a worthwhile difference in someone's life on your way up.

Marv Levy

COACH, POET, AND MORE

MARV LEVY WAS ELECTED TO THE PRO FOOTBALL HALL OF FAME in 2001. He began his head coaching career in the Canadian Football League and then broke into the NFL as head coach for the Kansas City Chiefs before he moved on to take the head coaching position for the Buffalo Bills where he won four American Football Conference Championships.

Rarely do we think of football coaches and poets in the same light, but Marv Levy is both. When I contacted him and asked for his thoughts on hindsight, he first complimented me on my writing accomplishments. I was humbled to know that Marv Levy had read books I had written. He just finished writing a 200-page book of his own poetry, and as his contribution to *Hindsight*, he wanted to share one of his poems as well as one of his favorite poems written by Edgar Guest.

PERSIST

By Marv Levy

There will always be ups and downs;
Ideas expressed by naught but clowns.
There will be countless ins and outs;

Firm opinions and plenty of doubts.
So let me be true to what I believe.
If it doesn't succeed I will not grieve.
Instead I'll give it renewed thought
And seek to profit from what I've been taught.
And even then, if I fail to make it,
I won't resort to trying to fake it.
I'll just go back at it once more
Since it is giving up that I abhor.
Bounce back I will with vigor anew.
I'll let no challenge knock me askew.
I'll go at it hard with all that I've got.
If it doesn't work out, quit I will not.
Never will I ever give in.
Being a quitter to me is a sin.
Instead, I will with surging inspiration
Go back at it again with full dedication.

IT COULDN'T BE DONE

By Edgar Guest

Somebody said that it couldn't be done
But he with a chuckle replied,
"Maybe it couldn't, but he would be one
Who wouldn't say so 'till he tried."
So he buckled right in with a bit of a grin
Never doubting or thinking to quit it.
And he started to sing as he tackled that thing
*That couldn't be done, and **he did it.***

I hope the next time you start to think of another person in a stereotypical or single-faceted manner, you'll remember a special poet who was a champion head football coach.

Jerry Lee Lewis

THE KILLER LIVES ON

JERRY LEE LEWIS HAS BEEN SINGING, RECORDING, TOURING, AND playing the best piano most people have ever heard for over 60 years with no end in sight. His recent album, *Last Man Standing*, has been acclaimed by critics as one of his best ever.

A new generation of fans are learning about Jerry Lee Lewis from the Broadway show entitled *The Million Dollar Quartet*, which chronicles one special time at Sun Records in Memphis when Elvis, Carl Perkins, Johnny Cash, and Jerry Lee Lewis all came together in the studio for one magical recording session.

As a very young man, I aspired to be a songwriter and actually wrote a dozen songs that were recorded on a demo that was sent to RCA Records in Nashville. Someone there thought enough of a couple of my tunes to invite me to Nashville for a meeting. Those songs never sold, but while I was in Nashville at RCA Records, they took me on a tour and showed me the studio where Jerry Lee Lewis had recorded most of his rock and roll hits in the 1950s. They have kept the studio much as it was a half-century ago, and Jerry Lee's piano is still there.

I have always been a believer in the old adage: *If you don't ask, the answer is no.* So I asked if I could go into that historic studio and play Jerry Lee Lewis's piano. It remains one of my fondest memories from my feeble songwriting and musical career.

Jerry Lee Lewis earned the nickname *The Killer* from some of his outrageous behavior when he first became a rock and roll superstar. His thoughts on hindsight are much like a great song lyric—very brief but powerful and poignant.

> *Ask God to guide you on all decisions, keeping your mind focused on your goal!*

The kind of focus Jerry Lee Lewis has demonstrated throughout the decades has carried him through the lowest valleys and over the highest mountain peaks, but he is still filling the seats and rocking the house.

Art Linkletter

WATCH WHERE YOU'RE GOING

AT A VERY YOUNG AGE, I WAS DIAGNOSED WITH A DISEASE THAT would result in my blindness. Shortly after the diagnosis, I was invited to a positive thinking rally which featured some of the greatest speakers of all time. Art Linkletter was among them. He was a marvelous platform speaker and was a tremendous force in the entertainment industry.

If you were around in the late 1950s and early 1960s, you probably remember watching *Art Linkletter's House Party* on television. Who could forget his interviews with children, during which he would ask them simple, innocent questions and often receive answers that brought to mind the phrase "out of the mouths of babes"? Mr. Linkletter, of course, turned that phrase into "Kids say the darndest things" and even wrote a book by the same title.

He wrote several other books as well, including *How to Be a Super Salesman, Yes, You Can!, Public Speaking for Private People*, and *Linkletter on Dynamic Selling*; but when I asked him to share his thoughts on hindsight and what he had learned, his reply had nothing to do with selling yourself or some product. It had to do with giving of yourself. I think you will enjoy this story.

For a good many years, I visited and spoke at the Braille Institute here in Los Angeles during their Christmas celebrations, and I know how much more joyful they make the holiday season. Occasionally, something happens to underscore the rewards that I have received from being a part of their programs.

About two years ago following one of these appearances, I was out having a Sunday joy ride with my family in Beverly Hills and inadvertently made a left-hand turn at an intersection without noticing that a man was on the curb with a white cane and a Seeing Eye dog.

He stepped off the curb, and even though I was proceeding slowly and slammed on my brakes immediately, he walked into the fender and fell down. Naturally, I was horrified at having caused a blind man to fall down and was relieved when he appeared to be all right. But right after, the thought of potential headlines occurred to me since, in these litigious days, any well-known person can be hauled through courts and the tabloids as a result of even a minor accident such as this one.

In assisting him to his feet and blurting out my profuse apologies, he stopped me by saying, "Aren't you Art Linkletter? I think I recognize your voice because two days ago you were entertaining us at the Braille Institute." I acknowledged that I was the same and apologized again, and he stopped me and said, "Don't worry, please, about this accident; you will have no problems with me. And even if you had run over me, what you do for us at Christmastime is worth so much that I would forgive almost anything you could do."

Talk about bread cast upon the waters!

He's right. You never know when one of your acts of kindness will come back to you in a timely, beneficial way.

There is another quote attributed to Mr. Linkletter that ties in with the idea of putting something in to get something out. Of course, we should never "give to get," but there are times when we need to give our best effort in order to achieve the success we are after.

People find gold in fields, veins, river beds, and pockets.
But wherever you find gold, it takes work to get it out.

Let's roll up our sleeves and get to work.

ULTIMATE HINDSIGHT

Bob Losure

FROM HEADLINE NEWS TO HINDSIGHT

I GREW UP IN TULSA, OKLAHOMA, AND AT THAT TIME WE HAD ONE news talk radio station that had one traffic reporter. They didn't have a traffic helicopter so when the lone traffic reporter, Bob Losure, reported a traffic jam somewhere in town, he was stuck in the middle of it. He was known then as the *KRMG Man on the Move.*

Bob did, indeed, move from traffic to news and from radio to local television to national television and finally to the anchor of *CNN Headline News* where he was broadcast worldwide for more than a decade.

After his great success at CNN, Bob moved back to Tulsa, Oklahoma, where we met and became friends. We have shared stories and advice over the years, and now I am pleased to give you just a glimpse of some of the wisdom Bob Losure has shared with me.

> *At an early age, I always got check marks on my report card right on the line between **always does** and **too often does not** when it came to following directions, and I'll confess it hasn't changed.*

My dad once told me that if I cut back 25 percent on rushing into decisions, and thought hard on what I was about to do, I would have a happier life. Boy was he right. Mistakes I've made in matrimony, investing money, and speaking my mind would probably not have happened as often if I had just slowed down.

There are times to act boldly and quickly—such as 1985 when I waited far too long to see a doctor about what turned out to be fast-growing testicular cancer. I nearly paid the ultimate price by waiting six weeks to have an examination. Three operations, three sessions of chemotherapy, and six months in and out of St. Francis Hospital in Tulsa, and I was back on my feet...mercifully.

There was a lesson even beyond surviving cancer in all that. No time to sit back and feel sorry for myself. Yes, the TV station where I'd worked for 10 years in Tulsa had replaced me on-the-air permanently. I had to hope some TV news director somewhere would take pity on me if nothing else. That man was Paul Amos, then Vice-President of News at CNN Headline News in Atlanta. I went there to audition in the fall of '85. My hair was coming out in clumps from the chemotherapy I was still receiving, but Paul's mother had battled cancer, and while he never mentioned that to me, I think he knew how hard I would work to prove worthy of CNN. He hired me, and I started an 11-year career in January of 1986 at what was then still referred to not as CNN but as The Chicken Noodle Network, working on the Headline News side.

Many times in the middle of the night at the CNN Center in downtown Atlanta, I was pleasantly surprised by how I kept my energy up for six, and sometimes eight, hours of sitting in that anchor chair reading 180 words a minute into a camera. I had the energy because I was passionate. Passionate not about thinking I was some kind of mini-celebrity at 2 a.m. on CNN but about reading national and international news with energy and accuracy that made the viewer want to hear more. And without passion for what we really want to do in life, what have we really got?

I have seen coffee shop waitresses who could have been psychologists, cashiers who could have been accountants. Often as I have found in traveling the country and speaking about fear of change, fear of taking a risk, fear of not overcoming adversity, I've seen people who have lost their passion for what they really should be doing with their lives. Finances have gotten them down, their health may have deteriorated, and maybe others who could have changed their paths have remained silent.

I tell others to do what I should be doing more often—caring for others and their day-to-day struggles. My 4th grade elementary speech teacher, John Kennedy, once told our class while giving us a particularly exhaustive test that "You will have disappointments in life. It's how you deal with them that matters." He was so right. If I simply gave up every time adversity knocked at my door, or I tried and failed to get a job, I wouldn't be me, and I wouldn't be any kind of inspiration to anyone else.

I was a very skinny, shy young man when my 10th grade English teacher, Sheila Parr, came up to me one day and asked if I would like to be in her journalism class. I know today how lucky I was to catch that train as it rolled into the station. I took a chance, put my passion for writing to work beginning with the student newspaper, then to the metropolitan dailies, radio news reporting and anchoring, TV reporting and anchoring, then global anchoring.

I had found what I was passionate about doing. And you know what? If tomorrow I develop a passion for growing plants and flowers, then I'll know it in my heart, and go full-speed ahead. And even if I'm not successful financially, I'll achieve what I was meant to do.

Sometimes it's easy to watch someone sitting in the spotlight with their makeup on and assume life has been easy for them. Bob Losure has faced more trials and tribulations than most people I know, and he has done it with a humility and grace that can inspire us all.

Harvey Mackay

SWIMMING WITH THE SHARKS

HARVEY MACKAY IS A COLLEAGUE AND MENTOR OF MINE. HE IS A fellow author, columnist, and member of the National Speakers Association, which is where I first came in contact with him. A lot of our peers think Harvey Mackay came from the old school. I like to think of Harvey as both old school and cutting edge.

His thoughts on hindsight range from sharing our fellow writer Robert Fulghum's wisdom about kindergarten, and then Harvey brings his own perspective on the rest of our lives and careers.

A FEW THINGS I LEARNED AFTER KINDERGARTEN

Several years ago, Robert Fulghum simplified the rules of life with a classic little gem, All I Really Needed to Know I Learned in Kindergarten: "Wisdom was not at the top of the graduate-school mountain but there in the sand pile of Sunday school." He covered all the basics for living a good life.

But the next 12 or 16 or 20 years of school that most of us were required to attend hold some mighty important lessons also. Especially if you plan to work for a living. It's not the dates and places and names, although those are significant. It's also the work ethic and habits that we formed that carry over into the everyday practice of our chosen occupations.

Remember those little reminders the really good teachers were always offering: Well, I'm a huge supporter of life-long learning, so if you didn't get the rules the first time around, I'll share some of them with you.

- *Pay attention. Knowing what's happening around you doesn't automatically happen. Putting the puzzle together isn't a gimme, either, if you've missed a few pieces. Depending on others for information is only as good as their attention span. It's up to you to stay alert.*

- *Take good notes. I've always said that pale ink is better than the most retentive memory. Remembering what happened in a meeting two weeks ago, which was sandwiched among thirteen other meetings on various topics, is difficult even if you possess an elephantine memory. If it's important enough to meet about, it's important enough to take notes on. Then, as a little homework, review your notes. You may find it amazing that you forgot a few details over time, but you'll be grateful for the memory jog.*

- *Be on time. Tardiness will affect your grade. When attendance is taken, make sure you're there. The early bird gets the worm, and all that. As Woody Allen said, "Eighty percent of success is showing up." This rule also applies to work deadlines. Get your projects finished on schedule, fill your customers' orders as promised, return calls and emails promptly, or plan to lose points. Otherwise, the "U" grade you get will not only stand for* **unsatisfactory** *but also* **unemployed***.*

- **Don't cut class**. *Everyone is entitled to vacation time and personal days, but be sure to use them wisely. The boss knows who's around and who can be counted on in a pinch. If you have a habit of sleeping late or taking off early to beat the traffic, you will never go to the head of the class.*

- **It's hard to learn with your mouth open**. *Be a good listener, don't interrupt. Try to really hear what's being said. Ask serious questions if you don't understand. While I'm not so sure there is no such thing as a dumb question, I am convinced that there are many good questions out there.*

- **Learn from your mistakes**. *Everyone makes mistakes; it's how you handle them that matters. You wouldn't err if you already knew everything. Try to think of mistakes as opportunities to improve.*

- **Don't be afraid to change your major**. *Should the day come that you lose your enthusiasm for your job or it just feels like work, you need to switch gears. Another favorite saying of mine* *is, "Find something you love to do, and you'll never work a day in your life." Think about how many hours you spend on the job, and then try to justify doing something you hate. Don't waste your talent. No amount of money is worth a job you can't stand.*

- **Check out extra-curricular activities.** *You need to find some balance between work and the rest of your life. Take a class, start a hobby, join a softball team, learn to bake bread, study a foreign language. Use the other side of your brain. An added benefit: you may learn something that enhances your job skills. And you had fun doing it!*

- **Don't let spring fever lead to the "Senior Slide."** *Slacking off gets you laid off. Think you can rest on your laurels? Don't get too comfortable. The quality of your work is a good indicator of your commitment to your job. Discipline yourself to get past the distractions.*

Mackay's Moral: *A student of life always does the homework.*

Now in his 80s, Harvey Mackay works harder than ever. He's not just managing what he has or things he's done in the past. He's learning about the future because he intends to be part of it.

Dan Marino

A QUARTERBACK WITH A CAUSE

DAN MARINO HAS BEEN INDUCTED INTO THE NFL HALL OF FAME. Sports fans and pundits often while away the hours arguing who was the best of all times. Any such debate or conversation about quarterbacks has to include the name Dan Marino.

He was drafted into the NFL in 1983 in what has been known as the "quarterback class." There were many great college quarterbacks entering the NFL that year, and Dan Marino was the last one selected in the first round. He went on to lead his Miami Dolphins to the playoffs 10 out of his 17 seasons in the NFL.

Like most great people I have met, when asked about hindsight or his advice on life, Dan spent most of his time talking about other people and good causes including our Narrative Television Network and very little time talking about himself.

As you know, I focus my efforts to provide programs and services for children, teens, and young adults with autism and other special needs. The Dan Marino Foundation, established in 1992, has grown, and the Dan Marino Center receives over 50,000 visits annually. In addition, we opened the doors in October 2013 for Marino

Campus, an educational and recreational facility for young adults ages 18 to 26 years old.

We know that the good work and contributions made through the Narrative Television Network will continue to enhance the lives of so many people. In June, I was the keynote speaker at the Family Café in Orlando with over 6,000 in attendance, and my message there would be one that can certainly be shared: "Don't ever let anyone tell you that you can't do something. You have to do the work, but don't listen to anyone who says you can't."

All quarterbacks lead their teams while on the field. Dan Marino can lead us all as we pursue a successful life.

Richard Marriott

A BRIDGE FROM SUCCESS TO SIGNIFICANCE

RICHARD MARRIOTT HAS BEEN AN INTEGRAL PART OF BUILDING and maintaining his family's hotel empire; much of his time, effort, and energy, however, are dedicated to his charitable Bridges project which helps young people with disabilities transition into the workplace.

As he uses his hindsight to look back on his life and career, he focuses on good work and good works.

The biggest realization we have come to in Bridges is that everyone has abilities, and if they can find a job that uses those abilities, they will be successful and happy. Almost everyone needs a helping hand to be successful in life.

Life Lessons: The Marriott journey has been a remarkable one—for the company and for the family. Corporately, it has its roots in the little nine-seat root beer stand that my folks opened in Washington, DC, in 1927; and achieved its latest milestone in the opening of our 4,000ᵗʰ hotel earlier this year—the flagship Washington Marriott Marquis—just a few blocks from where that root beer stand stood. Personally, that journey has very much shaped who I am and has provided some important lessons along the way.

I doubt if every lesson learned is contained in the following list, but I'd view these as some key guidelines to getting everything one can from life:

- *Recognize, nurture, and support the people around you, and they'll nurture and support you. The cliché "It takes a village" is well worn, but it is also true. People are the most important ingredient in most endeavors, in business, and in life. We all need each other to be the best that we can be, so reach out and build relationships every chance you get.*

- *Seek the opportunity that exists in every challenge. I do not minimize the fact that some face far more daunting challenges than others, but obstacles arise in every journey. Success can often be found not simply in overcoming the obstacle, but in discovering the possibility that lies within it and in building on that possibility.*

- *Set goals for yourself and then take action to achieve them. Each of these—setting goals and taking action—are central to all progress in life. But doing either one without the other isn't likely to get you very far for very long.*

- *Don't be afraid to fail. The likelihood is that you will not succeed all the time, but that doesn't mean that it isn't important to try. And when you do fail, pick yourself up and get right back at it. It's not that winners never fall down. It's that after they fall, they're the quickest to get back in the race.*

- *Finally, as my father used to preach, remember that success is never final. It's always important to celebrate and enjoy an achievement, but having met one objective, we need to be looking ahead to determine what we should be working toward next. In life, as in business, if we're standing still, we're probably falling behind.*

The name Marriott has come to stand for a certain standard throughout the industry and the world. We can all learn from Richard Marriott that standards of excellence are what we should strive for and what we will become known for.

ULTIMATE HINDSIGHT

Paula Marshall

A SLICE OF THE PIE

PAULA MARSHALL IS THE CEO OF THE BAMA PIE CORPORATION. If you think you've never heard of Paula or her products, you've most likely consumed a number of the products her company produces. The company was founded by her grandmother and grew under her father's leadership, but Paula has taken the organization to new levels.

In the 21st century, business leaders focus on two objectives—bagging the elephant and going to the Promised Land. Bagging the elephant means doing business with the giants such as Walmart and McDonalds. Paula counts both among her clients as well as many other elephants in the business world, and with her launch of Beijing Bama, she has taken her company to the Promised Land where I know she will continue to serve her ever-growing number of clients and consumers.

I am as impressed as anyone about Paula Marshall professionally, but even more important to me is the fact we have been friends for many years. We have mentored one another and drawn on our unique and differing perspectives. Paula is a top executive who manages people, money, and resources with excellence. I am an entrepreneur and like to focus on creating something out of nothing. Several years ago, we collaborated on a book entitled *The*

Executive Entrepreneur which marries the two areas of business expertise and focus.

Paula has reduced her hindsight to a series of power statements that can help us all.

> *Part of being a good leader is knowing that you don't have all the answers but finding out where you can get them and trusting the people who work for you.*
>
> *A savvy executive will envision the end result and then consider whether the steps to get there will merit the outcome.*
>
> *Being approachable nets far better results in terms of employee collaboration and productivity than being intimidating.*
>
> *Don't wait for chance or coincidence to determine your future. If starting a business is your dream, learn exactly what you need to know, and take the necessary steps to plan accordingly. A delayed dream that succeeds is far better than an impulsive one that fails.*
>
> *Being adaptable to the imperfections in others, rather than rigid about your own expectations, can lead to discovering their assets as well.*
>
> *Never sacrifice quality for quantity.*
>
> *At the end of the day, executives are human. We feel good about some decisions, bad about others. Inner peace comes with knowing that we did the best we could with the conditions and circumstances we had to work with.*

The next time you're in almost any restaurant that is a national chain, you will probably be consuming some of Paula's food. The next time you want to succeed at a greater level, remember to consume her advice.

ULTIMATE HINDSIGHT

Denny Matthews

THREE STRIKES TO SUCCESS

I GREW UP IN A TYPICAL NEIGHBORHOOD WITH ONE GLARING exception: The TV sportscaster in my hometown lived on the corner, two doors away from our home. Because Mr. Webber did the sports at 6:00 p.m. and 10:00 p.m. each evening, he was free during the day so could join in with the neighborhood boys in our football, baseball, and basketball games all summer long.

As a nine-year-old, I was convinced that the greatest job in the world had to be a sportscaster.

Then Mr. Webber got a so-called promotion and became the news anchor for the TV station. I couldn't understand why that was a promotion or what bad thing he must have done to lose his position as the sportscaster just to read the news each night.

These many years later, I still think being a sportscaster is one of the greatest jobs in the world.

Denny Matthews has been a broadcaster for the Kansas City Royals since the team's inception in 1969, and he's still going. He has been honored by the Baseball Hall of Fame. Drawing on his baseball experience and great success, he reduced his hindsight advice to three powerful strikes.

- *Know your abilities and interests, and apply that to your dreams and ambitions. Have confidence. Don't underestimate yourself.*

- *If you think you can, **or** if you think you can't, **you're right!***

- *Try to learn something and improve on something **every day.***

It is powerful when someone like Denny Matthews who has been at the top of his profession for over 40 years is still trying to improve every day. If it works for him, how can we do anything else?

Tim McCarver

MOVE OUT OF YOUR COMFORT ZONE

I REMEMBER MY SUMMERS WHEN I WAS IN ELEMENTARY SCHOOL. These were spent, in large part, listening to St. Louis Cardinal baseball on my transistor radio. I remember following every game on the radio and cheering for players I had never seen. One of my favorite players on the St. Louis Cardinals of my youth was Tim McCarver.

Being the catcher on a baseball team has to be one of the toughest jobs in sports. Even with all the protective armor, a catcher is the one who gets "taken out" when a player slides into home, and you know that has to hurt. Anyone who can endure that kind of abuse, year in and year out, must really be hooked on the game.

I think that describes Tim McCarver fairly accurately. He started out with the St. Louis Cardinals in 1959 and also played for the Philadelphia Phillies, the Montreal Expos, and the Boston Red Sox before retiring from the game in 1980.

Did I say retire? Tim McCarver didn't leave baseball. He became a sportscaster for the Phillies, the Mets, and ABC Sports before settling in with CBS Sports in 1990. In talking to me about success, he referred to his move from the Phillies to the Mets and shared one of the secrets of making it to the top.

> *In my professional life, the most naked I have been was when I moved from the Philadelphia Phillies to the New York Mets in 1983. I was very comfortable in Philadelphia but had always heard that New York is the place to be. While that is true, New York City can also be a very lonely place when you are away from your family and consumed in work; however, I traded the security of a life with nominal practical rewards for a life fraught with speculation and the roll of the dice.*
>
> *My confidence and professional staying power were certainly tested, but in looking back, it was worth the risk.*
>
> *In the sportscasting field, New York is the place to be; three of the four networks are based there. If you can cut it, the chance for opportunity is there.*

Once you have arrived at a place in your life that is satisfying and safe, it is tempting to stay right there. But if your dream is a little bigger than the opportunities being offered, sometimes you have to get out of the boat and swim for a distant shore.

Matthew McConaughey

KEEPING IT IN PERSPECTIVE

MATTHEW MCCONAUGHEY IS AN ACADEMY AWARD-WINNING leading man who is at the top of his game. He is respected by his peers and enjoyed by audiences around the world.

I was so delighted when he agreed to share some thoughts with me from his own hindsight, but my respect grew for him when he chose to focus his advice toward keeping success in perspective and respecting those around you.

*In 1995, I got my first big paycheck for an acting job: $48,500. **Schedule F** it was called, and I was so damn happy because I only had $2,600 to my name the day before. So, on location, I have a sweet guest house on the edge of a preserved national desert in Arizona, and I've got a maid to boot.*

*A friend of mine came over one night and asked me how I was doing, and I proceeded to tell her the many ways and reasons I was so happy at the time. "My job, my health, the big paycheck, this cool rental pad, a maid," I said. "A maid who even **irons and starches my blue jeans!**" I raved.*

My friend paused, slyly looked me sideways in the eye and said, "Well, that's cool…if you want your jeans pressed."

I suddenly got this blank look on my face and thought about my pressed jeans, not the fact that for the first time in my life I had someone who would press them, and I started chuckling.

She said, "What?" and I said, "You know what? You're right. I hate that crease in my jeans, that stiff starched line running from thigh to toe. I hate that line!"

*The next day, I asked my maid to stop starching and creasing my blue jeans, and since that day when I get offered **more** of anything, I ask myself if **more** is better. If I really want **more**.*

*So, next time you do something merely because you **can** for the first time, ask yourself **why** you're doing it and the **reason** for it. Do you really like it? Do you really want it?*

More is not always better, and I still don't like my jeans starched.

The next time you enjoy Matthew McConaughey playing a character in a movie, remember the wisdom and perspective of the man behind the role.

Lee Meriwether

BRING COLOR TO SOMEONE'S WORLD

GROWING UP, I KNEW LEE MERIWETHER AS MISS AMERICA, THE original *Cat Woman*, and a TV and movie star with many credits to her name. When we began casting *The Ultimate Gift* movie based on my novel, someone mentioned that Lee Meriwether would be a perfect Miss Hastings.

Miss Hastings is an integral part of my *Ultimate Gift* book series and movie trilogy. She supports the character, Mr. Hamilton, who is a focal point of each plot, but Miss Hastings often drives the emotion and the message behind the scenes. I was honored that Lee Meriwether wanted to play the role, and she has brought Miss Hastings to life in all the *Ultimate Gift* movies.

I remember arriving on the movie set for the first day of production. The esteemed actor Bill Cobbs was playing Mr. Hamilton, and Bill had just undergone some major surgery so was having a few challenges getting around and playing his part. Lee Meriwether was by his side every moment helping her fellow actor just as her character, Miss Hastings, supported Bill Cobbs' character, Mr. Hamilton, for decades. Lee Meriwether is, indeed, a great actress but when she plays someone like Miss Hastings who is loving and giving, I think it just comes naturally for her.

When I asked her to share her thoughts on success from her own hindsight, as I would expect of Lee Meriwether, she diverted the attention from herself and brought someone else into the spotlight.

There he was, standing by my hospital room door, bracing his small body on a single crutch. A blue-eyed, tousled-blond-haired, midsized, handsome boy of ten or so with a soft southern accent and an easy, quick smile. He had heard from the nurses down in pediatrics that I was in the hospital with hepatitis. Whether he knew who I was, I'm not sure, but I was a sick puppy in a downward spiral of depression. I had been three days away from opening in a play there in New Orleans, and they had replaced me with Dina Merrill.

He had a picture just for me that he had painted. It was a wonderful watercolor. Bright and happy, the scene was of his home. You could see it was filled with love. His family and a few animals were there, all going about their daily activities.

His name was Christian Guillot, and he was hoping the picture would cheer me up. It did, but not just for the artistry or for the caring his good heart was sharing.

It was in the picture itself that I realized the strength and courage of the young man before me.

Through this act, he made me stop feeling sorry for myself. From that morning, I started to improve. Now, I'm not saying this was any miracle, but I did have a new attitude to face my situation, and the doctor commented that I was fighting now, and that was helping.

I've kept in contact with Christian over the years. He's quite a celebrity in Louisiana.

My memory of that day in the hospital and of subsequent visits when we both received care at Ochners returns often. I thank the good Lord for giving me the chance to have met this amazing young man. I've saved that picture he painted, and, as always, I draw strength from his little self-portrait down in the corner: a blue-eyed, tousled-blond-haired young boy with just one leg.

The next time you see a TV show or movie starring Lee Meriwether, I hope you'll remember the powerful story she shared. If Lee is on the screen playing an evil or bad character, it's because she's a great actress. If she's playing a loving and wonderful character, it's because she's Lee Meriwether.

ULTIMATE HINDSIGHT

Matt Monger

FOOTBALL, FAITH, AND FINANCE

MANY PEOPLE KNOW MATT MONGER FROM HIS SEVEN YEARS IN the NFL where he played for the New York Jets and the Buffalo Bills. I first became aware of Matt Monger as I listened to Oklahoma State University football games on the radio. Matt was an All Star college player on some of the best teams the OSU Cowboys have ever had.

I didn't meet Matt Monger in person until after his football career had ended. You've probably heard it said of someone who is both trusted and respected, "I would trust that person with my life savings." To a great extent, that's what I have done for many years and continue to do with Matt Monger.

After his successful football career, Matt joined one of the major Wall Street firms and began helping people manage their money. Matt attacked the world of finance the same way he attacked the world of football—with intensity, motivation, and effort.

As many readers of my other books or weekly syndicated columns know, I am a very early riser, getting up each day at 4:00 a.m. When I began working with Matt Monger as my financial advisor, I was delighted to learn that Matt is an early-morning person as well. He is in the office most days between four and five in the morning, and we talk virtually every day before the sun rises.

Those who have read my *Millionaire Map* book know that I started with nothing, and through many of the principles that others have shared in this book, I became a multimillionaire. Any financial advisor in the country would want my account today, but Matt Monger took me on as a client when I had almost nothing to invest.

For several years, I struggled to reach a goal that was a financial milestone. Finance is like football in that we keep score. I remember one morning I called Matt to check on the totals and the portfolio, and he answered the phone by inquiring, "Are you dressed?" I was bewildered and told him I was in my bathrobe, and it was only 4:30 in the morning.

Matt responded, "Put some clothes on and answer the front door."

I hurriedly dressed and went to the front door, and there was Matt Monger with the printouts of all my financial statements showing that I had reached my financial goal. I believe during Matt's football career, in addition to being a player, he learned how to be a great coach and cheerleader.

He shared some powerful thoughts from his own hindsight.

A mentor taught me I should press on in faith, knowing that faith is where success begins. I embrace the vision of several past coaches and tell myself I will not be denied. I will not fail. Yet I question if it is really as simple as making a decision to win and following a formula.

Faith does create motivation which leads to commitment. Commitment produces hard work and preparation. These yield successful efforts which produce confidence. Confidence leads to more faith, and so the cycle is complete and continues. The process will often take you closer to achieving your goal.

But most important is the one thing they often neglect to tell you: That faith must have an object. You must have faith in something.

We place our faith in our abilities, our talents, our effort, and oddly enough sometimes in faith, to which I encourage all to realize we are merely reflections of the Master we serve, erroneously and arrogantly convinced that we are self-managing ourselves. This is essential because at the end of the day we each have to ask, "Do I want to accomplish my goals or the goals of the Master I serve?" If I accomplish my goals, I will swell with pride yet remain unfulfilled. If I accomplish the goals of my Master, I will be exactly where I am supposed to be, experiencing complete joy and success.

Psalm 37:4 states it clearly, in that if I will put my faith in and pursue Him, He will give me the direction and desire to accomplish.

Where is your faith?

If you're going to succeed financially or in any other area of life, you've got to have what I call "your dream team" around you. These are mentors and advisors who can help you get from where you are to where you want to be. Matt Monger is that kind of mentor and advisor, but he's also a great friend.

ULTIMATE HINDSIGHT

Russell Myers

BORN TO DO IT

WHEN RUSSELL MYERS WAS WORKING FOR HALLMARK AND trying desperately hard to break into the "funny papers," a friend of his suggested that he do a comic strip featuring a witch. He drew a character that he called *Broom-Hilda*, and that feisty little witch has been flying high ever since her first appearance in 1970.

When Russell Myers wrote to me to share his thoughts for this book, he let me in on a little secret: Comic strip characters have a mind of their own. Sometimes they write their own dialogue. Even if you create something, sometimes you have no control over what you have created. In Russell Myers' case, it seems to have worked out for the best.

I want to share his entire letter with you. I know you will enjoy it as much as you enjoy his work.

> *There are many rewards to drawing a nationally-syndi-cated comic strip. One nice one is that people send you money every month, and you can eat food and have a house and shoes and sox [sic]. Another is that sometimes somebody says that they enjoy what you do. It's impossible not to smile when that happens.*

But I submit that most of us in this funny little business believe that we do what we do because we were born to do it. Each and every day, we are doing what we are supposed to, and it's fun. To sit in a room and write and draw little people that hop about on the page and say and do funny things, many of which surprise me as much as they do you, is a treat.

I have trouble believing that any IRS agent or fish cleaner enjoys himself on the job. I have trouble believing that any cartoonist doesn't.

Imagine being paid to have fun. Russell Myers just proved that it is possible.

Jack Nicklaus

THE GOLDEN BEAR

AS A BLIND PERSON MYSELF WHO HAD SIGHT FOR THE FIRST PART of my life, I treasure certain visual images in my memories. In 1986, my sight had deteriorated to the point that I had to get within a few inches of the television screen to watch anything. I had given up on most TV and movie viewing, but when the 1986 Masters Golf Tournament came on network television, I had to watch it.

I had grown up around the game of golf as my father played a lot and, at one point, had taught me the game. During the '60s and '70s, Dad and I enjoyed watching golf on TV together, and there was no one who dominated the sport more during those decades than Jack Nicklaus; but by 1986, Mr. Nicklaus was 46 years old and hadn't won a major tournament in several years.

The announcers were polite and respectful when they showed Jack Nicklaus playing as he was a five-time former Masters champion, but they, along with the thousands watching in the gallery and millions watching on TV around the world, gave Jack Nicklaus virtually no realistic chance to win. In the history of golf, no 46-year-old player had ever won a major tournament, and virtually everyone thought it was impossible except for Jack Nicklaus.

After two rounds on Thursday and Friday, Jack Nicklaus had actually made the cut, which meant he was in the upper half of the competitors so would get to compete on Saturday and Sunday. He stayed in the middle of the pack on Saturday, but Sunday, the final round of the Masters, was pure magic.

Jack's son, Jackie, was caddying for him during the tournament, and I remember the two of them crouching over a putt with Jackie helping his father read the slope of the green because, as the announcers put it, "Jack's eyesight isn't what it used to be." I was watching the action with my failing eyesight, a few inches from the TV screen, so Jack Nicklaus went from great to heroic to monumental on that day.

He kept picking up strokes and overtaking the competitors ahead of him in the tournament as the day wore on. The announcers started to take him seriously, and the galleries of fans watching the tournament live gathered around Jack Nicklaus in record numbers. Everyone sensed something historic might happen.

When he got to the 16th hole, he was within striking distance of the players in front of him. The 16th at Augusta is a difficult hole, and on that day, the pin placement or hole location was in a very challenging spot on the green. The best players in the world had been having trouble with that hole all day.

I remember the sight of Mr. Nicklaus standing on the green with his son, discussing the shot. Once they had determined how to play the hole, Jack Nicklaus didn't hesitate. He just stepped up to the ball and hit it. He didn't even look to see where it had gone but just bent down to pick up his tee and head for the green.

His son, Jackie, could be heard on the TV broadcast saying, "I hope it's close."

Those in the gallery and a few of us very close to the TV set could hear Jack Nicklaus say as he walked away, "It will be close."

The ball landed on the green and settled about three feet from the hole. Jack Nicklaus knocked it in for a birdie and went on to win that tournament. It was his sixth Masters championship—a feat no one has ever equaled.

He has virtually rewritten the golf record books and has amassed career statistics and numbers that may never be duplicated, but on that one day, he hit one shot I will never forget.

Years later, I had lost the rest of my sight and continued to follow golf tournaments on satellite radio. You can imagine my excitement the day an envelope arrived at my office from none other than Jack Nicklaus. He had read one of my books and complimented me on it. Since that day, I have sent him each of my books, and I feel privileged that we have stayed in touch and are friends. I think of him often and remember that one shot.

I believe all of us have opportunities each day to do something monumental if we will just take advantage of the situation. It becomes possible when you have an attitude like Jack Nicklaus shares in his hindsight.

> *Golf is a game of respect and sportsmanship; we have to respect its traditions and its rules. Success depends almost entirely on how effectively you learn to manage the game's two ultimate adversaries: the course and yourself. Sometimes the biggest problem is in your head. You've got to believe you can play a shot instead of wondering where your next bad shot is coming from.*
>
> *Confidence is the most important single factor in this game, and no matter how great your natural talent,*

there is only one way to obtain and sustain it: work. Focus on remedies, not faults.

Concentration is a fine antidote to anxiety. Resolve never to quit, never to give up, no matter what the situation.

People don't want to go to the dump and have a picnic; they want to go out to a beautiful place and enjoy their day. And so, I think our job is to try to take the environment, take what the good Lord has given us, and expand it, without destroying it.

Never forget the power and the potential that you have each day as you go through your tasks and routines. We all have the chance to be heroic if we will do the right thing next and the next thing right.

Justice Sandra Day O'Connor

IT'S QUALITY THAT COUNTS

SANDRA DAY O'CONNOR WAS NOT WELL KNOWN OUTSIDE JUDICIAL circles until that day in 1981 when she became the first woman to be confirmed to the U.S. Supreme Court. A moderate conservative, she rose through the ranks, first as an assistant attorney general, majority leader of the Arizona Senate (the first U.S. woman to hold such a post), and a Superior Court judge.

In answering my request for her viewpoint on success, Justice O'Connor sent me a transcript of an address she delivered to a college graduating class. Some of the points she was driving home to these new graduates are points we would do well to take.

> *The person who really impacts on this world is, as has always been the case, not an institution, not a committee, and not a person who just happens to have a title; rather, it is the truly qualitative individual. The qualitative individual **does** matter in this quantitative world of ours, now as ever.*

Justice O'Connor went on to quote a passage from the Talmud that is also noteworthy:

> *In every age, there comes a time when leadership suddenly comes forth to meet the needs of the hour. And so*

*there is no man who does not find his time, and there is
no hour that does not have its leader.*

In explaining this passage, Justice O'Connor said:

*Each of us, in our own individual lives and crises, will
have a time to lead. Whether we will lead only a family, or a handful of friends, and when and how we will
lead, is up to us, our views, and our talents. ...The very
nature of humanity and society, regardless of its size or
complexity, will always turn on the act of the individual
and, therefore, on the quality of the individual.*

You might scoff when you hear someone say, "One person can
make a difference." But if a Supreme Court justice believes it can
happen, I think we should start believing it, too.

Tom Osborne

COACHING FOR SUCCESS

TOM OSBORNE HAS SERVED THREE TERMS IN THE UNITED STATES House of Representatives, but he will always be remembered as the head coach of the Nebraska Cornhuskers where he led the team for over 25 years, winning three national championships and being inducted into the College Hall of Fame.

Growing up in Oklahoma and following the beloved Oklahoma Sooners, I remember Tom Osborne as the coach who led the dreaded Nebraska team into all the fierce rivalry games with Oklahoma. All of the games were classics, but one of the Oklahoma/Nebraska games has actually become known by the experts as "the game of the century."

Being a great coach, Tom Osborne draws on the wisdom of others and brings his own slant to that wisdom.

> *The advice I often pass on to young people does not originate from me. Rather, it is a quote from Warren Buffett who often tells young people to "invest in yourself." This type of investment has to do with acquiring as much education as possible, surrounding oneself with people of wisdom and sound character, and engaging in activities which produce physical, intellectual, and spiritual growth.*

Nebraska is a relatively small state with respect to population, but any state that has Warren Buffett and Tom Osborne as residents doesn't have to take a backseat to anyone.

Dr. Mehmet Oz

A BALANCED PRESCRIPTION

DR. OZ IS AN EMINENT PHYSICIAN WIDELY RESPECTED BY HIS colleagues, but he has become the doctor to the masses due to his numerous television appearances. As usual, his advice is balanced and practical. His hindsight brings us a prescription for living a healthy, happy, and successful life.

My advice for those just beginning their journey to success would be to have the goal of a healthy living philosophy—which should be to achieve and maintain physical and mental wellness. This can be achieved with a healthy diet, exercise, a strong social life, and the occasional indulgence. Diet and exercise keeps the body healthy and can prevent disabling diseases like heart disease and diabetes. Additionally, exercise boosts endorphins, a hormone in the body that promotes happiness and can decrease depression. Exercising 30 minutes per day for 5 days a week should be enough to feel the benefits. Another thing that is really important is having a strong social network with supporting family and friends. Feeling loved and loving others can promote a sense of belonging, increase self-worth, and feelings of security. All of these support wellness, and when your mind and body are healthy, you can achieve anything!

Here in the 21st century, we deal with medical breakthroughs and miracles that would have seemed like science fiction just a few years ago, but before we look to space-age medicine, it's good to take Dr. Oz's down-to-earth advice on living well.

Ara Parseghian

TIMELESS PRINCIPLES BRING TIMELY SUCCESS

ARA PARASEGHIAN WILL ALWAYS BE KNOWN AS THE HEAD COACH of the storied Notre Dame Fighting Irish football team. Few people will remember that when Coach Parseghian showed up in South Bend to take over the program, Notre Dame had suffered through five straight losing seasons. In his 11-year career as head coach, Notre Dame never had a losing season and won two national championships. He has a lot of hindsight to draw upon and a lot of success to recommend him.

> *I have been out of coaching over 40 years, but one of the sayings we had would certainly apply. "Adversity has the effect of eliciting talents that, under prosperous circumstances, would have remained dormant."*

Notre Dame football is the stuff of which legends are made, but there are no legends without victories, and there are no victories without success principles to guide us.

ULTIMATE HINDSIGHT

T. Boone Pickens

COMPETE TO WIN

T. BOONE PICKENS HAS OVER A HALF CENTURY OF EXPERIENCE IN business, but he remains on the cutting edge of technology and global influence. One need look no further than the news to see that T. Boone Pickens is called upon for his experience relating to the past and his insight relating to the future.

He wanted me to share this with you:

> *More than eight decades on this earth has taught me a thing or two. Here are a few that I hope might be meaningful, no matter what the individual circumstances:*
>
> ***America remains the greatest country in the world.*** *There's more opportunity for success today than ever.*
>
> ***Don't think competition is bad, but play by the rules.*** *I love to compete and win. I don't want the other guy to do badly; I just want to do a little better than he does.*
>
> ***Learn to analyze well.*** *Assess the risks and the prospective awards, and keep it simple. Be willing to make decisions. That's the most important quality in a good leader: Avoid the "Ready-aim-aim-aim" syndrome. You have to be willing to fire.*

Learn from mistakes. That's not just a cliché. Remember the doors that smashed your fingers the first time, and be more careful the next trip through.

Embrace change. Although older people are generally threatened by change, young people love me because I embrace change rather than running from it.

Great advice comes from people who have been to the mountaintop, and even greater advice comes from those who are using their perspective from the summit to look toward the next mountain.

Gary Player

PUT PROBLEMS IN THEIR PLACE

GARY PLAYER HAS ALWAYS STOOD FOR THE VERY BEST THINGS that golf embodies. He has the ability to be a total gentleman and a fierce competitor at the same time. I was very pleased when the Senior PGA Tour was developed. It gave a whole new generation an opportunity to learn about golf and life from Gary Player.

After entering the U.S. Professional Golfers Association in 1955, he went on to win 31 tournaments, including the British Open, the Masters, the U.S. PGA, the U.S. Open, the South African Open (he was born in South Africa), the Australian Open, and the World Series of Golf. He was only the third player to win golf's Grand Slam.

By anyone's definition, this man is a winner, but as he told me, he has his ups and downs like everyone else. Listen to what he's learned.

> *Everyone has problems! It is part of our mortal experience. We have troubles to teach us patience, humility, and longsuffering, and most important, to bring us closer to our faith; however, it is not the problems that count*

but the manner in which we handle them. Our attitude is one of the most important fundamental aspects of our lives.

We have the choice to make the best or the worst of any situation.

Many years ago, I was fortunate to read Norman Vincent Peale's book, The Power of Positive Thinking, and Dale Carnegie's book, How to Win Friends and Influence People. These excellent books helped me to achieve a good outlook, a positive approach, and always to maintain a good sense of humor. "Laugh and the world laughs with you; cry and you cry alone."

My great faith is most important in my life and in that of my family. This faith has given me courage to endure setbacks. Faith brings an inner peace and joy that is truly the peace of God that passes all understanding.... We need to keep God's Ten Commandments; they can always show us the way we must live. We need to hold fast to the "Iron Rod," that being the Word of God.

Mark Twain once said, "Golf is a good walk spoiled." I think he would have seen the game in a whole new light if he'd had the chance to tee off with Gary Player.

Nido Qubein

STUDENT AND EDUCATOR

NIDO QUBEIN IS A FELLOW MEMBER OF THE NATIONAL SPEAKERS Association, a colleague, and a friend. He is president of High Point University and has honored me greatly by inviting me to speak to his staff, his faculty, and most importantly, his students.

He has a hard-won perspective on life and valuable hindsight.

I wish I'd known that relevance, not excellence, is what brings one the most advancement in life. Being excellent in all we do is a good thing. Being relevant to the teams we work with gets attention, or merit, because enlightened self-interest inspires people to want more of you when they need you in their lives. It isn't only about rendering value; but, rather, about interpreting your value in useful ways so people want what you have.

All my life I've known that the more strengths we have, the better off we'll be. But is that true in these competitive and ever-changing times? Strengths alone won't do it. It's our differences that make us substantially more purposeful. I'm not saying strengths are not important. They are just not enough. They may be replicable. Even commonplace. This global platform on which we

199

are asked to perform demands us to be differentiated in meaningful ways.

While I've always understood the value of lifelong learning, only recently did I delve into exploring the difference between having a fixed mindset (what you know and do well) with a growth mindset. So many studies show empirical evidence that our minds are expansive when we allow them to be. Someone said if you'll learn one new piece of information every single second, it'll take you three million years to completely use the capacity of your brain. Wow!

Nido Qubein is teaching more than he ever has, but he's still learning every day.

Jerry Rhome

PAIN, PERSISTENCE, AND POSSIBILITIES

JERRY RHOME HAS BEEN INVOLVED WITH FOOTBALL FOR OVER HALF a century as a player and as a coach. He excelled in the high school, college, and pro ranks. His advice is time-tested, and his hindsight can make us all champions.

In 1955, I broke my femur in half just above the knee and was in a full body cast for five months. They utilized the first metal screw ever used. As a result, my leg is one-and-one-half inches shorter than the other, but my spine grew crooked so it made me level. I have lots of pain now at 72 years old, but I am in excellent shape and still work with young football players.

I retired from 33 years in the NFL and three years coaching at Tulsa. Fifty yards from the high school field where we practiced was the spot I wrapped my leg around a small tree "racing" on a bicycle! I was barely 13 years old. Four years later, I was a high school All American.

I outworked everyone, had a plan, and stuck with it—running, jumping rope, obstacle courses, etc.—and I played three sports. So I was playing something every day including boxing and golf although basketball, baseball, and football were my main sports.

My motto? Never quit! Never give up! And outwork your competition and opponent. Always play smart! Keep your mouth shut unless it is positive or you are encouraging your teammates. Don't blame others, and certainly give your opponent credit for their victory. Give credit to your teammates and coaches. And keep your mouth shut about your own accomplishments.

Jerry Rhome reminds us all that pain fades, losses turn into lessons, and only victories endure.

Oral Roberts

FOLLOW YOUR CALLING

IN *WHO'S WHO*, ORAL ROBERTS' PROFESSION IS GIVEN SIMPLY AS "clergyman," but he did much more in his lifetime. He pastored churches, conducted evangelistic crusades around the world, founded and served as president of the university that bears his name, taught, published magazines, appeared regularly on radio and television, and founded a retirement center and a medical and research center.

Controversy seemed to follow Oral Roberts wherever he went, but he knew from the beginning that the message he preached would never be a popular one to everyone who heard it. His parents, however, taught him early to obey God. God, Himself, he had said, spoke to him when he was a teenager. At the time, he was gravely ill with tuberculosis and was on his way to a tent meeting where an evangelist would pray for him. "Son," God said, "I am going to heal you, and you are going to take My healing power to your generation." Oral Roberts was, indeed, healed and did, indeed, do his best to fulfill the calling God had placed on his life.

Like so many successful men, Oral Roberts had a lot to overcome. His family was very poor. He was a stutterer who had to endure the taunts of his classmates. But he had dreams and was determined to rise above his situation. For a time, he couldn't decide between preaching and becoming a lawyer. His parents' influence and his own faith—and the conviction that he had to obey God—helped him to make his choice. He never looked back.

"I'm an evangelist first and last," he said when I interviewed him for television. No one who heard him preach can doubt that.

During some of his ministry's best years, he suffered some of his greatest personal tragedies. His older daughter and son-in-law died in a plane crash, and one of his sons committed suicide. What brought him through such terrible times of testing was, of course, his strong faith in God.

When it comes to the church, some say that success is measured by the size of the building, the number of members, the variety of programs offered, and the reputation of the pastor. For a man like Oral Roberts, however, whose work went so far beyond the traditional church structure, filling pews and earning the world's acclaim are not how God measures success. It all still comes down to obedience.

He went on to say in our interview:

> As I stand here today, I would do it all over again. I'd take every step. I'd make every journey. I'd fly every mile. I'd try to climb every mountain. I'd do it all over again. I wouldn't change a thing. I'd lay it upon me and upon you and upon everybody who will listen.
>
> I'd tell everybody to listen to God's voice.

If you don't do what you know in your heart you are supposed to do, you will never find success.

Kenny Rogers

ICING ON THE CAKE

I HAVE HAD THE OPPORTUNITY OF SEEING KENNY ROGERS SEVERAL times in concert. Through all of his personal and professional challenges, he has never done a bad show. Whether you like his work or not, when you leave the concert hall, you know that you have just experienced the best that Kenny Rogers has to offer.

He began playing music in high school, dropped out of college to join a jazz trio, and was with *The New Christy Minstrels* before he formed the group that put him on the music map— *Kenny Rogers and The First Edition*. After a nine-year run with the group, he went solo, scoring a Grammy with a country song called *Lucille*. The following year, he struck gold with a toe-tapping number called *The Gambler*, a song that spawned several television movies.

Kenny Roberts looks like the kind of man who has been there, done that, and lived to tell about it...and he is. Just listen to what he has to say about success:

> *I consider success to be relative. When I was a kid, I lived in a federal housing project in Houston, Texas. To my knowledge, the most my father ever made was $75 a week. He was a wonderful man who lived during very tough times.*

I think that as children we all strive to improve on the accomplishments of our parents. I remember feeling successful the first week that I made more money than he did. While it was not much, it represented success to me.

If young people can learn to set difficult yet attainable goals, they establish themselves, in their own minds, as achievers.

Success, however, does not guarantee you happiness. Interestingly enough, if you ask most people who are truly successful, I think that very few would say that their happiest moments were when they made their most money, but rather, when they felt the real possibility of achieving their dream.

I was told, and I believe, that a person needs three things to be happy: someone to love, something to do, and something to look forward to.

Happiness is just that simple. Success...simply the icing on the cake.

It is obvious that making music and entertaining audiences is what makes Kenny Rogers happy. If happiness brings us success, I wish him many years of happiness to come as he entertains us all.

Cesar Romero

NECESSITY CAN BE THE MOTHER OF JOY

CESAR ROMERO HAD A DISTINGUISHED CAREER IN THEATRE AND films. Like many actors, however, his crowning achievement came in the guise of a television role—as the Joker on the *Batman* series.

Late in his life, he agreed to an interview with me. What we can learn from what he said is that sometimes, the dream finds *you*. Thinking back over the years, Cesar Romero said:

> *Most of all, I am humbled and thankful for the career and the friends I have made. I started in this business simply as a way to support my family, but through the necessity of working, I found a true joy in my career.*
>
> *As I look back, I realize it was the greatest thing that ever happened to me.*

Sometimes you do what you have to do. And sometimes, if you're lucky, the thing you have to do becomes the thing you want to do more than any other. Open your heart and your mind to the possibilities.

ULTIMATE HINDSIGHT

Donald Rumsfeld

DEFENSE AND SUCCESS

DONALD RUMSFELD IS BEST KNOWN FOR HAVING TWICE SERVED as the Secretary of Defense for the United States. His wisdom and experience have led us through some difficult times globally.

As a great leader and student, he draws on the wisdom of others to build his own hindsight.

> *My most recent book, Rumsfeld's Rules, includes some of the lessons and wisdom I gathered over my years in public service and business. I have included some of the rules below:*
>
> *"People respond in direct proportion to the extent you reach out to them." —Vice President Nelson Rockefeller.*
>
> *"Discipline yourself and others won't need to." —Coach John Wooden.*
>
> *"Victory is never final. Defeat is never fatal. It is courage that counts." —Sir Winston Churchill.*
>
> *"The most important things in life you cannot see: civility, justice, courage, peace." —Unknown.*

We live in a world where it is possible for us to destroy not only our enemies but the entire planet; therefore, wisdom dictates that, whenever possible, peace is the best defense with wisdom and hindsight as our guide.

Leon Russell

ROCK AND ROLL RESPECT

LEON RUSSELL IS A MEMBER OF THE ROCK AND ROLL HALL OF Fame. He has played on hundreds of albums as a studio musician for artists ranging from Frank Sinatra to the Beach Boys. Then after launching his own career, he became a bona fide rock star in every sense of the word.

I met Leon Russell when I was only 13 years old. I was washing dishes in an Italian restaurant where Leon was holding his 30th birthday party. I paid one of the bus boys $5.00, which was half a night's pay, so I could just wander out in the dining room and look at Leon Russell. Years later, I told him that story, and I remember him asking me if it was worth it. I assured him it was worth it then as well as now to spend some time with a legend and a rock star.

His hindsight brings us an amazingly down-to-earth perspective.

In this country, we are conditioned to think that we can always do better. The downside of this, unfortunately, is that sometimes people are not satisfied with the hand that they are dealt. They feel that they should want more, forever.

I saw an interesting documentary about a neurosurgeon in England. The filmmakers were suggesting that national medicine in England did not offer him the rewards he deserved. If he worked in America, he could have a bigger house, a number of automobiles, and many other luxuries and a much higher salary.

His answer was, "I have a very nice place to live, a fine auto; in fact, I have everything I need for a wonderful life. What would I do with a big house that I don't need, more than one car that I don't need. I have an opportunity to help people with my work. That is my principle desire. To have all those things that you mentioned would just be a distraction."

You can make your own happiness.

I remember asking Leon Russell when he really hit the big time. His answer has remained with me to this day. "I hit the big time in my career when I quit thinking small time in my mind."

I have told millions of people in my speeches at arena events that you "Change your life when you change your mind." Leon believed it and proved it long before I ever thought of it.

Dr. Paul Schervish

PEACE OF MIND

FOR SEVERAL YEARS, DR. PAUL SCHERVISH AND I HAVE SERVED AS co-honorary chairmen of the National Financial Literacy Campaign. I met Paul in 2007 when we were making *The Ultimate Gift* movie based on my novel. He served as an advisor regarding issues of estate planning and philanthropy.

Dr. Paul Schervish is Professor of Sociology and Director of the Center on Wealth and Philanthropy (CWP) at Boston College, and he served as a Fulbright Professor in Philanthropy at University College, Cork, Ireland.

His hindsight focuses on the battle we all face between fear and serenity.

> *I grew up in Detroit, resigned to a perilous future. I assumed I was not going to live to be 45 years old. The ever-impending prospect of nuclear war with the Soviet Union traumatized me with nuclear anxiety. And if we skirted a nuclear holocaust, I would die young from a heart attack. Heart attacks killed both of my grandfathers well before I was born; and my father was hospitalized with heart disease on and off for years from the time he was 45. All this was accompanied by a financial collapse in our family that reinforced a wretched*

insecurity. I remember Sister Josine asking each of us 8th graders what aspirations we harbored for 15 years down the road. When it was my turn, I respectfully told her I didn't know. I didn't want to tell her that I had no future to plot. My existence would be truncated either from a bomb bursting in the sky or my heart bursting in my breast. The 13 days of the Cuban Missile Crisis and my father's continuing heart failure simply confirmed the dread that had become a familiar but unwelcome guest in the basement of my soul. Such burdens made my life heavy laden—one ruled by a cycle of imposed duty, moral failure, and expiation.

Looking back, I now recognize how those years incited my quest for inner peace and a way to milk precious morsels of happiness from each scarce hour. What I learned, I do not yet live fully. But I know it to be true, and that it is a worthy message for others. My schooling came from St. Ignatius of Loyola, the founder of the Jesuit religious order. What he taught he learned from life. Those of us striving to go from good to better should distrust and dismiss anxiety, fear, and doubt as the work of the evil spirit slyly eating away our spirit under the guise of good. As I sometimes put it, complying with self-denigration and the tutelage of guilt is ingesting poison from a milk bottle. Instead, according to Ignatius's spiritual psychology, we should trust and treasure the peace, courage, and happiness even though we are tempted to see this as giving in, being too soft on ourselves, or being morally lax. This is the milk we mistakenly deem to be poison.

Learning to discern the subtle workings of the evil spirit versus the workings of the good spirit is easier in theory *than in practice. But our life depends on learning the dispositions, decisions, and deeds of inspiration rather than those propelled by fear and guilt. The will of God, I have learned from a wise teacher, is found not in what guilt tells us to do, not in what the churches tell us to do, not in what others tell us to do, and not in what is the hardest or even the easiest thing to do. The will of God is found in what we are inspired to do. When spiritual instructions enter our conscience, explains Ignatius, like water splatting against a stone, we are to dismiss them. When fervent purposes arrive softly and tenderly like water dripping into a sponge, we are to pursue the directions they counsel. This reversal of our familiar self-deprecating spiritual psychology is the path to salvation—not away from it. Allowing ourselves to find and follow what inspires us opens the flow of life-giving energy of compassion toward oneself and others. This knowledge is not too great for us; it is "already on our lips and in our hearts" as the Book of Deuteronomy says. We discover this path to loving kindness toward our self and others whenever we craft our daily version of the spiritual reversal that Ignatius sets forth. We need to implement this reversal straightaway and not wait for the hindsight attributed to the old woman who lamented, "If I had it to do over, I would have eaten more ice cream and fewer peas." Let the ice cream parlors of the world be opened.*

Dr. Paul Schervish has helped countless people focus on generosity and philanthropy. His words here are a gift to us all on how to get the most out of each moment in this life.

ULTIMATE HINDSIGHT

Max Schmeling

TODAY IS WHAT COUNTS

BOXERS GET A LOT OF BAD PRESS. (WITNESS A HIGH-PROFILE EAR-biting incident.) That hasn't always been the case. In the 1920s and 1930s, a German boxer named Max Schmeling caught the imagination—and the admiration—of the world.

In his memoirs, Schmeling said, "It was a time that wanted heroes. As a boxer, I was a symbol."

He was also Germany's only world heavyweight boxing champion. As such, he was a man on whom many Germans pinned their hopes and dreams.

He won the title in 1930 against an opponent named Jack Sharkey. Two years later, Schmeling lost the rematch, but immortality was just around the corner. In 1936, he knocked out the previously-unbeaten Joe Louis in what became known as the "Sensation of the Century."

In a 1938 rematch with Joe Louis, he was knocked out in the first round. Rather than bemoan his loss, however, he looked at the bright side and said, "A victory against Louis might have set me up as the Nazis' model Aryan."

Throughout his career, Max Schmeling was seen as an honest man without pretensions. Many wanted to use the boxer for their own purposes—including Hitler's Nazis—but he remained true to himself. When his career ended, he bought a farm, studied business, and obtained a production license from a major soft drink company.

It would be tempting in his ninth decade (as he was in 1997 when we connected) to sit around and dwell on what had happened 60 years earlier—to revisit the glory days, if only in his mind. But Max Schmeling had always been, if anything, a forward thinker:

> *I don't really think about the past. What matters is the present. And a huge interest in the future.*

They say that wisdom comes with age, but they don't say you can't cut a few corners and learn from someone else's experience. In a letter from Mr. Schmeling, he told me what a privilege it had been to pass along his wisdom through this book. I think the lesson that Max Schmeling learned—live in the moment and look forward to tomorrow—is one we should all take advantage of right now.

Dr. Robert Schuller

SHARPEN YOUR FOCUS

THE INTERVIEWS AND MATERIAL FOR THIS BOOK TOOK OVER A quarter of a century to gather. As I sat down to compile *Hindsight*, some of the celebrities and personalities involved were still living and making their mark in the world while some had passed away, leaving a powerful legacy. It was poignant that just as we were finishing the manuscript for the book you are now reading, Reverend Robert Schuller passed away.

He was a great influence on my life and career. He changed the world and left it a better place.

As founder and senior minister of the Crystal Cathedral in Garden Grove, California, Dr. Robert Schuller was one of the most visible ministers in America. His *Hour of Power* television program was on the air for nearly three decades, and he wrote more than two dozen books with titles such as *You Can Become the Person You Want To Be* and *Tough Times Never Last, but Tough People Do.*

Dr. Schuller was, for many years, an inspiration to me and to millions of people around the world. He became a mentor and a friend. He was kind enough to endorse my first book, *You Don't Have To Be Blind To See*, and to submit some of his thoughts for this book. What he said about sight emphasizes, for me, the need to focus on what you're doing if you want to be successful.

Sight does not happen in the eye, even as hearing does not happen in the ear.

This is obvious. Sighted persons do not "see" many things in front of them. They only "see" what they are focused on, thinking about, aware of in their mind and spirit.

So the person who is really blind is the person who is distracted from reality by anxieties or fears or other negative thoughts that...keep the center of his mental consciousness from really reading the thought that has come into mind.

Until you learn to rely on your brain, rather than on what your eyes and your ears are telling you, you will never be able to "see" things as they truly are. And if you can't "see" exactly what is going on, you will find yourself making educated guesses about how to proceed. It's silly to stumble in the dark when the world's greatest computer—your brain—is at your disposal.

It's like they say: A mind is a terrible thing to waste. Use yours to fuel your drive to success.

Charles Schwab

SEEK OUT NEW SOLUTIONS

CHARLES SCHWAB IS THE CHAIRMAN OF THE BROKERAGE HOUSE that bears his name. He is also the author of *How to Be Your Own Stockbroker*.

More importantly, he founded the Parents' Educational Resource Center (PERC), a nonprofit agency that provides support and guidance for parents of children with learning differences, and is the founding chairman of All Kinds of Minds, a nonprofit institute that promotes understanding and the best possible care of children with learning differences.

You see, Charles Schwab was diagnosed with dyslexia, a condition that makes reading and writing difficult. His son faces the challenge of dyslexia, too. Mr. Schwab founded PERC as a result of the experiences he and his wife had as they were trying to find help for their son.

When someone you love is challenged in some way, you want to do everything you can for him. I'm glad people like Charles Schwab don't stop there. I'm glad they take the time to look around and say, "Does anyone else have this problem? How can I help?"

Observe the way that Charles Schwab views what some would consider a negative condition.

As a person who has struggled with reading problems all of my life, I believe that people who learn differently look at the world from unique perspectives. Many of our students are highly creative, visualizing solutions that might not occur to the rest of us. By identifying what gets in the way of learning for students, we are able to nurture their strengths, improve their self-esteem, and teach them the skills they will need to become our inventors, leaders, and entrepreneurs.

As parents, clinicians, and teachers, we have the opportunity—and the responsibility—to positively influence our children's lives.

Charles Schwab didn't let dyslexia prevent him from succeeding in the world of finance. Happily, his success is turning out to be someone else's good fortune as well.

Vin Scully

LET'S PLAY BALL

I AM A HUGE FAN OF BASEBALL GAMES BROADCAST ON THE RADIO. Many people would think it's because I'm blind, but I think baseball and radio were made for each other, and listening is the best way to enjoy the game.

There are a few constants in our world, and Vin Scully broadcasting the Dodgers games seems to be one of them. He has been bringing the action to Dodger fans since 1950, which was before the Dodgers left Brooklyn for the West Coast. Sixty-five years later and still going, he has a passion for the game that is evident in his work.

Vin Scully has been named to the Baseball Hall of Fame as well as the Radio Hall of Fame. His brief thoughts on hindsight reflect his passion for what he does and the fact that he's always looking forward.

Over the past six decades, I have truly enjoyed the relationship I have had with Dodger fans all around the world. As I have said many times, it is the roar of the crowd that keeps me excited and gives me goose bumps before every game, and it is my honor to broadcast Dodger baseball into your homes. I hope I will see you at the ballpark soon, and I thank you for your continued support of the Dodgers.

I hope on a lazy, beautiful summer day you can find a quiet spot somewhere and enjoy Vin Scully painting the pictures that will bring you a baseball game. You will hear passion and professionalism from a gentleman who is still convinced that the best is yet to come.

Frank Sinatra

HE DID IT HIS WAY

YOU'VE HEARD IT SAID THAT SOMEONE "NEEDS NO INTRODUCTION," which is what is generally said before they give someone an introduction. Frank Sinatra needs no introduction but certainly deserves one.

I had the opportunity to meet and interview Frank Sinatra late in his life when he was doing a concert with the Dallas Symphony. We met at the hotel where he and his entourage were staying. They had blocked off the top two floors of the hotel for Mr. Sinatra. The police had cordoned off the streets in front of the hotel, and there were news helicopters circling the building.

I was in awe when I first met Frank Sinatra and quipped, "Mr. Sinatra, you've created quite a stir here in Dallas."

He seemed bewildered and asked one of his people, "Do you know what he's talking about?"

His longtime friend and bodyguard responded, "Yeah, boss. I know what he's talking about, but you don't."

It dawned on me that for over a half century, he had never been anywhere that wasn't in total turmoil because Frank Sinatra was the center of the hurricane his entire life.

Frank Sinatra was an Academy Award-winning actor and one of the top recording artists of all times, but his stardom went far beyond these accolades. Frank Sinatra was a force that impacted his industry and the world around him in a way that we may never see again.

Here are a few thoughts Mr. Sinatra had drawing on his own hindsight.

The best revenge is massive success.

I would like to be remembered as a man who had a wonderful time living life, a man who had good friends, fine family—and I don't think I could ask for anything more than that, actually. People often remark that I'm pretty lucky. Luck is only important in so far as getting the chance to sell yourself at the right moment. After that, you've got to have talent and know how to use it. Throughout my career, if I have done anything, I have paid attention to every note and every word I sing—if I respect the song. If I cannot project this to a listener, I fail.

I'm gonna live 'til I die.

When I concluded my interview with Frank Sinatra, he walked with me toward the elevator and left me with a phrase he was fond of saying instead of good-bye. "I hope you live to be 100 years old, and the last thing you hear is me singing you a song."

Steve Spurrier

A TALE OF A COACH

STEVE SPURRIER WAS A TWO-TIME ALL AMERICAN COLLEGE quarterback and Heisman Trophy winner. He had a successful professional career as a quarterback and then, as a college coach, won a national championship before he went on to coach in the NFL.

Today, he coaches again in the college ranks which is his first love, and as you will see from the tale he offers below, above all, he views himself in hindsight as a coach.

THE COACH

And in those days, behold, there came through the gates of the campus a coach from afar off, and it came to pass as the seasons went by he won games and championships in abundance.

And in that land where there used to be losers, and they used to spend their days adding to the alibi sheets: Mightily were they astonished. They said one to the other, "How in the world doth he doeth, and how doth he have so much luck?"

And it came to pass that many were gathered in the corridors, and a soothsayer came among them. And they spoke and questioned him saying, "How is it that this coach has accomplished the impossible?"

*Whereupon the soothsayer made the answer: "He of whom you speak is one fierce competitor. He riseth in the morning and goeth forth full of confidence. He complaineth not, neither doth he know despair. He maketh solid plans and doggedly doth he pursueth them. While ye gather here and say one to the other, 'Verily, this is not a perfect situation,' he hath convinced his people that nothing can stoppeth them. And when the eleventh hour cometh, he needeth no alibis. He knoweth his job inside and out, and they that would defeat him, they lose. Rivals say unto him, 'Nay,' when he cometh in, yet when he goeth forth, he hath their names in the column that is marked **victory**.*

*"He taketh with him the three angels 'Enthusiasm,' 'Determination,' and 'Persistence' and worketh with a smile on his face. **Verily I say unto you, go and do likewise.**"*

Jim, I try my best to be this coach!

Steve Spurrier's best efforts have made him a champion and have made those he coaches champions.

Catherine Mary Stewart

A TRIO OF TRUTH

CATHERINE MARY STEWART IS A GREAT ENTERTAINER. LIKE MANY moviegoers, I first became aware of her in the comedy classic *Weekend at Bernie's*.

When my novel, *A Christmas Snow*, was turned into a movie, I was ecstatic when Catherine Mary Stewart agreed to play the lead role. Later, we were asked to turn that movie into a Broadway-style musical, and it played over 100 performances with Catherine Mary Stewart singing, dancing, and entertaining audiences. Making movies and doing live theatre is a lot of hard work. The glamor comes out in the performance, but there's a lot of effort and pain that goes into making a seemingly-effortless show possible.

Cathy is a true professional and a friend. She offers us all some powerful hindsight wisdom.

> *Life is a journey to be sure. Looking back, there are things I wish I had known when my journey began. Here are three that I know to be true.*
>
> 1. *Embrace and celebrate your differences, whatever they may be. Differences are what make each of us interesting and unique. If you look at those*

who lead successful, fulfilling lives, you inevitably find that they have carved a path that is true to who they really are and what they are passionate about.

2. *Set goals and work toward them 110 percent. Other doors may open along the way, and your path may change. That is OK. It's a good thing. Leave yourself open to new possibilities. Find a mentor, work hard, and follow your passion.*

3. *Never, **ever**, let anyone tell you, "You can't." Surround yourself with people who are supportive and believe in you. Follow your dreams and **believe** in yourself. If you believe in yourself, others will, too.*

Catherine Mary Stewart has proven herself as an actress, singer, dancer, and all-around performer. She pursues her passion, makes it look easy, and always has fun.

George Stovall

A FAMILY TRADITION

I HAVE RECEIVED FAR MORE NOTORIETY, ACCLAIM, FAME, AND fortune for sharing messages through my books, movies, speeches, and columns than I deserve. Most of the people in this book have earned their hindsight wisdom through trial, tribulation, and hard work. Much of my message came from my family and still does today. The sources of this wisdom would obviously include my mother, my grandmothers, and others, but for this offering, I will focus upon George Stovall, which is the name of my father, my grandfather, and my brother.

These men taught me much of what I know from what they did more than what they said; however, I grew up with some enduring statements that have given me hindsight to live by.

> *If you're not 10 minutes early, you're late.*
>
> *If you don't have time to do it right, when are you going to have time to do it over?*
>
> *If you can't pay for it now, what makes you think you can pay for it later?*
>
> *Always do your best.*

My grandfather taught me lessons through the way he grew things in his garden. My father taught me through the way he managed and still deals with people. My brother continues to teach me through the way he visualizes and builds buildings. Remember the people in your world who taught you through what they said and, more importantly, through what they did.

Make them proud.

Barbra Streisand

A STAR IS BORN

BARBRA STREISAND IS THE BESTSELLING AMERICAN FEMALE recording artist of all time. Her honors include an Emmy, an Oscar, and more gold records than any other recording artist. She has mastered stage, screen, and the music industry for five decades.

Few people have seen the world from the perch Barbra Streisand enjoys, and this gives her tremendous hindsight.

There is nothing more important in life than love.

Doubt can motivate you, so don't be afraid of it. Confidence and doubt are at the two ends of the scale, and you need both. They balance each other out. I've been called many names like perfectionist, difficult, and obsessive. I think it takes obsession, takes searching for the details for any artist to be good. You have to discover you, what you do, and trust it. There's always a part of you that remains a child, no matter how mature you get, how sophisticated, or how weary.

I arrived in Hollywood without having my nose fixed, my teeth capped, or my name changed. That is very gratifying to me.

Barbra Streisand might be challenging to work with, but the final results are always worth the effort.

ULTIMATE
HINDSIGHT

Coach Eddie Sutton

A LEGENDARY FRIEND

GROWING UP IN OKLAHOMA, I KNEW COACH EDDIE SUTTON AS the leader of the Oklahoma State University Cowboys basketball team. Then one day I had the great fortune to have him drop by our office to meet me. We found we had a lot in common, and everyone at the Narrative Television Network began looking forward to the periodic unannounced visits from Coach Sutton. He remains a valued mentor and friend to this day.

Coach Sutton was the first major college head coach to take four separate teams to the NCAA tournament. His squads made it to the final four twice, and he is one of only eight head coaches in history to amass over 800 victories.

He has the hindsight of a leader who built champions.

Over the years, I learned that the best team doesn't always win. The best-prepared team wins. If we're playing a team that is not as good as us, we have to remember the fundamentals; and if we are playing a team that is more talented than we are, we have to always remember we can win. Upsets can happen. It has happened to me. You just try to practice hard and sell your players on the fact that we have done everything we can for the preparation of this team. We all realize that they are a little bit better than we are, but that doesn't mean we can't upset them. If we play five games, they will probably beat us four times; but if we are going to play one game, we have to do everything to play over our heads.

That goes back to practice and making sure you have done everything you feel like you need to do. When we go out to play a game, we are going out with the idea that we're going to win. They are going to have to play over their heads to beat us.

There is so much involved in mental attitude when it comes to playing a game like basketball. You have to make sure you have prepared them in every way in practice sessions, and then you take the attitude that we can beat these guys. It may be hard, but we can do it if we play like we're capable.

When you're young, you think you know everything, and you really don't know everything. I think later in your career with all the experience you should be able to coach much better than when you were young. I look back now, and we had some losses, but we were prepared as a team, and I was prepared as a coach, and psychologically, we were ready to win.

Things have not always been easy, convenient, or smooth for Eddie Sutton. He has dealt with trials and tribulations but emerged victorious and maintained a sense of grace and gratitude.

Alex Trebek

BEYOND *JEOPARDY!*

As SOMEONE WHO OWNS AND OPERATES AN EMMY AWARD-WINNING television network, I would have to admit that TV is too often the "wasteland" it has been described to be. Much of the game show landscape on television has little or no redeeming value. *Jeopardy!* is the exception. The contestants are quick, intelligent, and well-informed scholars. Many high-profile people I know and respect are regular viewers of *Jeopardy!*

For over 30 years, Alex Trebek has brought knowledge and information into people's homes. This gives him a unique hindsight.

> *For a person like myself who has benefited from a remarkable series of good luck breaks in his career, the prospect of giving advice is a daunting one. I tell people all the time that a good education and a kind heart will be an enormous help in life, but there is more.*
>
> *If I had to condense into a very brief sound-bite that which I believe to be a most important bit of advice, it would be this: "Wear the other man's shoes."*

The format of *Jeopardy!* that Alex Trebek hosts gives the answers, and contestants have to discern the questions. Hindsight and wisdom are much the same. You must know where you want to go before you decide how to get there.

ULTIMATE HINDSIGHT

Donald Trump

BEING *THE DONALD*

I'VE HAD THE PRIVILEGE TO WORK WITH DONALD TRUMP ON several projects. Despite his reputation, Donald Trump is polite, prompt, and professional in everything he does. I always think of him as stamping the suffix "-est" onto everything he does. His projects are the tallest, biggest, costliest, and always the best they can be.

He draws from his hindsight he gained from his father's example.

I was fortunate to have a very solid foundation with my family and with my education as well. My father, Fred C. Trump, was a great mentor, and he told me to "know everything you can about what you're doing," which is advice I have followed. I was and have always been thorough.

What I learned later, after a financial downturn that was substantial, is that keeping your focus intact is of utmost importance. After surviving this difficult phase and coming back to be far more successful than before, I had time to reflect on what had happened, and it became clear to me—I had lost my focus. Sounds simple, but I would like to emphasize how much it matters.

Most people—and newspapers—were convinced I was finished, done for, gone forever. They were wrong, but making a comeback wasn't easy.

As I regained my focus, and my finances, I realized that maintaining a momentum was also critical to continued success. I had lost my momentum to a certain extent, which is what helps your achievement process to get you somewhere. When you are working with both focus and momentum, great results will follow. I wish I had paid more attention to these two factors then, and I certainly do now. I can tell you that it's a powerful combination.

Donald Trump is one of a kind, and there is much about success, enthusiasm, and excellence we can learn from him.

Ted Turner

LEND A HAND

SINCE THE DAY I LAUNCHED MY BUSINESS MORE THAN A QUARTER century ago, Ted Turner has been a mentor, a colleague, and a friend.

People thought Ted Turner was crazy when he proposed a 24-hour-a-day news channel. No one thinks that any more. *CNN Headline News* has leapfrogged over the competition with its coverage of late-breaking news.

As owner of the Atlanta Braves baseball team and the creator of three other cable TV networks, Ted Turner is a man who has definitely made his mark in the world. I'm happy to say that he has also been a tremendous encouragement to all of us at the Narrative Television Network. As we were seeking to do something new and unique, it was nice to follow a trail that had been blazed by a true pioneer like Ted Turner. He was gracious enough to endorse my first book, *You Don't Have To Be Blind To See*, and I'm glad to share part of a letter he wrote to me a short time after NTN went on the air.

Man should be judged by the deeds done to help his fellow man.

All of us have handicaps of one sort or another, and it is important that we lend a hand to each other so we can share the gifts we have been given.

Regardless of how busy we get in our daily lives, we must take time out to identify areas and ways in which we can help others. Christmas is a common time for this, but people should give of themselves year-'round.

This letter was written five days before Christmas—a time of year when most busy executives are not even in their offices, much less dictating letters to the new kid on the block. I would say that in writing this letter to us, and the letter he wrote two years later to congratulate us on winning our Emmy, Ted Turner was demonstrating that if you want to get ahead, you need to pay attention. You need to be aware of what others are doing, applaud their efforts, acknowledge their successes, and encourage them in their pursuits. When we all help one another, everybody wins.

The Most Reverend Desmond M. Tutu

YOU ARE LOVED

IT TAKES COURAGE TO STAND UP FOR YOUR BELIEFS. NO ONE KNOWS this better than Archbishop Tutu. It was in the late 1970s that this relatively-unknown bishop moved to the front of the anti-apartheid movement in South Africa. Recommending economic sanctions against his country and other nonviolent means of change, he was highly deserving of the Nobel Peace Prize that was awarded to him in 1984. Apartheid in South Africa has all but disappeared as we face the 21st century. Despite his international fame, however, Archbishop Tutu hasn't lost sight of what's most important.

He wrote to me:

So many of us suffer from the success/achievement/rat-race syndrome which says you matter only because you have made it. Most of us think that this attitude carries over into our relationship with God, that God loves us because we are lovable, we deserve to be loved, and we have made it by impressing God. The truth, the Good News, is that God loves me. Period. That is the most fundamental truth about me, about you. It is a free gift, unearned, undeserved.

God loves me not because I am lovable. I am lovable because God loves me. That is what gives me my worth, and nothing can change it.

Words to live by.

Ken Venturi

BEAT THE HEAT

ONE OF MY FAVORITE WEEKEND ACTIVITIES WHEN I'M AT HOME or traveling is enjoying a golf tournament on television. Because I am unable to see, the commentators are the most important aspect of the broadcast. Ken Venturi was my favorite. Not only was he a great commentator, he was a former champion who brought the same winning attitude to his work.

Golf was not Ken Venturi's first career choice. He thought he would become a dentist and play golf for fun. Instead, he turned pro in 1956 and proceeded to have four outstanding years. In 1961, however, he hit a slump that made him the invisible man in professional golf.

Then came 1964. Suffering from heat exhaustion, he nonetheless managed to win the U.S. Open. For this inspiring feat, he was named "Sportsman of the Year" by *Sports Illustrated*, and PGA Player of the Year. End of the story? Not hardly. Shortly after his dramatic victory, he developed a rare circulatory and nerve ailment in his hands that forced him into surgery and therapy. Determination brought him back to the tour where he regained his style and continued to play good golf for the rest of his career.

His new career, commentating, seems like a natural choice unless you know that he had to overcome stuttering to make the grade. So, you see, some successes are hard-won.

When I asked Ken Venturi to contribute to a book, he sent me a lot of information about one of his favorite charities, *Guiding Eyes for the Blind*. It's an organization he has supported for many years. In fact, each year there's a *Ken Venturi Guiding Eyes Classic*, a golf charity benefit that raises funds to train guide dogs.

He also sent me a copy of an interview he did with *PGA Magazine*. It includes a story that tells a lot about this successful man's character.

When asked to name the best golf course he ever played, Ken Venturi said this:

I would choose Cypress Point. I used to caddie there. The chefs used to help me out when I was a kid and give me fried chicken for lunch. And the caddies would always help me out. I was just 14 or 15. And I never forgot that.

I went back there after having won the U.S. Open, and they all said, "Ohhh, the big shot is here. The big boy. We thought you'd forget us now because you won the Open."

I said, "Are you kidding me? You guys? Would I forget you?" And the caddies gathered around me while I opened the trunk of my car; I had brought a whole bunch of fried chicken. And I said, "Now you can have lunch on me." And I had also iced down some Dom Perignon. And the caddies and I sat there and had fried chicken and Dom Perignon.

Explaining why he returned to Cypress Point that day, Ken Venturi gave the credit to his father.

When I told him I wanted to be somebody, he said, "I will always pray that you will be somebody. But I will pray more that you never forget where you came from."

He proved that he had a good memory, and I believe he also had a good attitude about life. I think it was the key to his success. As he told *PGA Magazine*:

I don't believe you have to be better than everybody else. I believe you have to be better than you ever thought you could be. I only lasted ten and a half-years on the Tour…. I feel that, in that time, I did the very best I could.

That's all that any of us can do.

ULTIMATE
HINDSIGHT

Dick Vitale

BE ENTHUSIASTIC, BABY!

DICK VITALE HAS BEEN A SUCCESSFUL COACH IN BOTH COLLEGE and professional basketball. He has authored nine books and appeared in several movies. He is best known, of course, for putting the "mad" in March Madness via his enthusiastic antics during college basketball broadcasts.

He shares some of his wit and wisdom from his hindsight.

> I have a very simple philosophy for life that I would like to share. I firmly believe in a theory that **passion + work ethic + good decision making in your life = win the game of life!**
>
> I have always felt that people who have a sense of pride and passion in what they believe in usually have a positive attitude in dealing with the everyday problems that they are confronted with. To me, it is vital to have a daily plan and move in a positive manner to execute each goal that you have set out to achieve. Many people have goals, and I believe in goal setting. But to me, the most important plan is: What is your **commitment** to make your goal a reality?

249

Thanks for asking me to share some insights on things that I firmly believe in and have utilized in my personal and professional life.

You are awesome baby with a capital A!

The next time you're enjoying a basketball broadcast and listening to the wild man, Dickie V, remember the success principles he offers, and enjoy the game.

Dr. Denis Waitley

BELIEVE IT...SEE IT...HAVE IT

FEW PEOPLE HAVE INFLUENCED MY LIFE LIKE DR. DENIS WAITLEY. He has been a shining example of excellence his entire life.

As a Blue Angel pilot, through his work as a psychologist with the returning POWs, and now as a bestselling author and a member of the Platform Speakers Hall of Fame, Dr. Waitley's message of hope has never changed. He encouraged me early on as a motivational speaker and was the catalyst who got me started on my first book. (He wrote the foreword to *You Don't Have To Be Blind To See*.) We've share the platform together and worked on television together, so I'm proud to include a few of his words of wisdom in this book.

I agree wholeheartedly with his philosophy.

> *The world tells us not to believe it until you see it. I know that you'll see it when you believe it.*
>
> *You can envision a bigger and more personally-fulfilling destiny for your life. And what you begin to see, you can begin to have.*

What Dr. Waitley is telling us to do, in essence, is to get rid of that voice inside our heads that says, "I can't succeed," and replace it with the voice that says, "I *can* succeed and I *am* succeeding!" When you start to see yourself in your mind as you *can be*, as a success, it won't be long before the person you dream (and believe) you can be will emerge. Keep telling yourself that you have *already arrived*, and see if that doesn't inspire you to make that conviction a visible reality.

Dr. Ruth Westheimer

DON'T JUDGE A BOOK BY ITS COVER

FEW PEOPLE HAVE EVER KNOWN THE RECOGNITION AND NOTORIETY that has come to Dr. Ruth Westheimer. Nearly everyone is aware of her books and of her work on television and radio, but few people know the real Dr. Ruth. We have had the opportunity to work together at several conventions and press conferences. She has always been a powerful encouragement to me and to everyone around her.

I remember, in 1991, a cable TV network announced that Dr. Ruth would be handling some of their broadcasts from the Democratic and Republican convention floors. She and I were at a press conference the next day when an uninformed reporter attacked her for getting involved in the broadcast of a political convention. When he said that having Dr. Ruth do such a broadcast would turn the entire election into a joke, Ruth calmly responded:

> *As someone who lost both of my parents in a concentration camp and grew up as an exiled prisoner myself, I think I understand the power and the value of a free society as well as anyone.*

Dr. Ruth reminds all of us that the freedoms we have make everything possible. No matter what tragedies you've suffered in your personal life, you can rise above them and make your own place in the world.

James Whitmore

TREASURE THE ADVENTURE

IN 1947, ACTOR JAMES WHITMORE WAS NAMED MOST PROMISING Newcomer. It turned out to be a prophetic award. He gave a number of notable performances on Broadway, and his movie work resulted in two Academy Award nominations. Some of you might remember him as the convict with the bird in his pocket in *The Shawshank Redemption*.

When he had half a century of work under his belt, James Whitmore looked back with pride on his contributions to the entertainment industry. This is what this gifted actor wrote when I asked him about hindsight:

> *After 75 years as an occupant of this planet earth, I have only this to say: Life is the most precious gift ever given.*
>
> *It knows not of good or ill. If we treat it with love and respect, in ourselves and in others, it will return to us fulfillment.*
>
> *The American Indians said of it, "Thou shall acknowledge the wonder."*
>
> *Both life and death are part of the same great adventure.*

As so many of the people in this book have said, it all comes down to attitude. If you believe the glass is half full, you are a lot more likely to succeed at whatever you try and to find happiness in the pursuit.

Andy Williams

SURROUND YOURSELF WITH WHAT YOU LOVE

ANDY WILLIAMS BECAME SYNONYMOUS WITH THE HOLIDAY season for millions of people around the world. I had been to his theatre in Branson, Missouri on several occasions and enjoyed his Christmas performance as a kickoff to our family's holiday celebration.

Long before he built his theatre, he built a reputation in the music business as a singer of love songs. His 17 gold albums, Emmy Awards, and Grammy Awards were appropriate honors for the man who gave us *Moon River, Days of Wine and Roses, Born Free*, and the theme songs from the movies *Love Story* and *The Godfather*, among many others.

I had the opportunity to interview him in a beautiful apartment he had built right behind the stage of his appropriately-named Moon River Theatre. I observed that, in much the same way that the holiday season is about gathering friends and family and things we care about around us, Mr. Williams created a life for himself that emphasized the things that were important to him and that brought him happiness, peace, and joy. "Happiness, I think, is really the most important thing," he told me.

And I'm happy here in Branson. I've got a lovely wife, two wonderful dogs, a home that I like very much, and this theatre. And I live on a golf course, and I like to play golf. So I've got just about everything around me that I really love.

In the long run, success is not measured in dollars and cents. Money helps, but being at peace with yourself and with those you love is of much more value.

Kemmons Wilson

ROOM IN THE INN

KEMMONS WILSON HAS BOUGHT COUNTLESS NUMBERS OF MY books and movies to share with his friends, family, and colleagues across the country. He has hired me to speak at several corporate, community, and charity events. He oversees the vast Holiday Inn hotel empire that his father founded and does so with an eye to success, significance, and service.

His hindsight spans several generations of family wisdom.

Things I Wish I Had Known When I Started Out—Hindsight

Nobody has it all figured out.

Know that we are the answer to nothing. The world will continue to turn even without our commentary or involvement.

People don't care how much you know until they know how much you care.

Time is everything to a relationship...hurry is the death of a relationship.

The greatest human temptation is to settle for too little.

If you are scared of criticism, you will go to your grave accomplishing nothing.

The only thing that "likes" change is a wet baby. Change is inevitable so be prepared.

Trust is the one quality that cannot be acquired. It must be earned.

The greatest test of a person's worth is their character.

Understand that the choices you make in life are paramount. They will follow you everywhere you go.

Every great accomplishment is an accumulation of many little things.

The only disability in life is a bad attitude. A good attitude costs nothing.

A dollar bill doesn't come with instructions, so you better know how to handle it.

There needs to be a consistency between your beliefs and your behavior.

Evil does not announce itself. It comes like a thief in the night.

The more you help others, the more help you will receive.

Don't be afraid to be the one who loves the other the most.

Always be looking for someone whose life you can make better.

Take risks and do not be afraid to fail.

Good judgement comes from experience, and experience comes from bad judgement and mistakes.

More people fail from lack of purpose than lack of talent. The world is full of smart, lazy, uncommitted people. Have great passion and strategic purpose in your life.

Always choose opportunity over security in your career.

*Know that there is no future in any job. The future lies in the **person** who holds the job.*

*"I love you; I'm sorry; Please forgive" are the most powerful statements in the world. We need to know **how** and **when** to use them.*

When it is all said and done, in the end, it boils down to Faith...Family...Friends.

Kemmons Wilson teaches us that you don't need to separate your business life from your family life or your service to others. If we are to succeed, we do so in every area of life.

ULTIMATE HINDSIGHT

John Wooden

THE WIZARD OF WESTWOOD

COACH JOHN WOODEN HAS SET NCAA CHAMPIONSHIP RECORDS that many feel will never be broken. He has been given every sports honor, award, and Hall of Fame induction that exists.

One of the great days in my personal and professional life was the day Coach John Wooden called my office to introduce himself, compliment me on one of my books, and have me autograph books for some of his friends and former players.

The term *legend* is often used too casually in our world, but Coach John Wooden was a legend, and his legacy lives on through everyone he touched in his almost 100 years of life. I was proud to count him among my friends and rarely go through a day without thinking about him and what he would say or do in a given situation. His success on the basketball court is unparalleled, and his success as a man was even greater.

His hindsight remains priceless.

> *Talent is God-given. Be humble. Fame is man-given. Be grateful. Conceit is self-given. Be careful.*
>
> *Things turn out best for the people who make the best of the way things turn out.*

If you're not making mistakes, then you're not doing anything. I'm positive that a doer makes mistakes.

It's the little details that are vital. Little things make big things happen.

Success is peace of mind, which is a direct result of self-satisfaction in knowing you did your best to become the best you are capable of becoming.

Be more concerned with your character than your reputation because your character is what you really are while your reputation is merely what others think you are.

Whatever you do in life, surround yourself with smart people who'll argue with you.

Do not let what you cannot do interfere with what you can do.

You can't let praise or criticism get to you. It's a weakness to get caught up in either one.

Never mistake activity for achievement.

The day Coach Wooden died, I felt a great loss, but when we have friends and mentors who leave their mark on us, they're never really gone.

Zig Ziglar

THE LAST ARE FIRST

IN ANY ALPHABETICAL LISTING, SUCH AS IN THIS BOOK, ZIG ZIGLAR is generally listed last. It's the way he would have wanted it as he spent his life putting everyone else first. Zig was an encouragement to me as a fellow speaker, author, and businessperson, but even more, he was a friend.

Zig had a faith and enthusiasm that impacted everyone around him. His words live on and will change lives for generations to come.

Positive thinking will let you do everything better than negative thinking will.

Your attitude, not your aptitude, will determine your altitude.

People often say that motivation doesn't last. Well, neither does bathing—that's why we recommend it daily.

The foundation stones for a balanced success are honesty, character, integrity, faith, love, and loyalty.

You can make positive deposits in your own economy every day by reading and listening to powerful, positive, life-changing content and by associating with encouraging and hope-building people.

Be grateful for what you have and stop complaining. It bores everybody else, does you no good, and doesn't solve any problems.

When you encourage others, you—in the process—are encouraged because you're making a commitment and difference in that person's life. Encouragement really does make a difference.

You can have everything in life you want if you will just help other people get what they want.

Time can be an ally or an enemy. What it becomes depends entirely upon you, your goals, and your determination to use every available minute.

Zig Ziglar's books, videos, and speeches were among the most impactful in the profession because they weren't just words, thoughts, or ideas to Zig. They were his life.

ABOUT JIM STOVALL

IN SPITE OF BLINDNESS, JIM STOVALL HAS BEEN A NATIONAL OLYMPIC weightlifting champion, a successful investment broker, the president of the Emmy Award-winning Narrative Television Network, and a highly sought-after author and platform speaker. He is the author of 30 books, including the bestseller, *The Ultimate Gift*, which is now a major motion picture from 20th Century Fox starring James Garner and Abigail Breslin. Three of his other novels have also been made into movies with two more in production.

Steve Forbes, president and CEO of *Forbes* magazine, says, "Jim Stovall is one of the most extraordinary men of our era."

For his work in making television accessible to our nation's 13 million blind and visually impaired people, the President's Committee on Equal Opportunity selected Jim Stovall as the Entrepreneur of the Year. Jim Stovall has been featured in *The Wall Street Journal, Forbes* magazine, *USA Today*, and has been seen on *Good Morning America, CNN,* and *CBS Evening News.* He was also chosen as the International Humanitarian of the Year, joining Jimmy Carter, Nancy Reagan, and Mother Teresa as recipients of this honor.

Jim Stovall can be reached at 918-627-1000 or Jim@JimStovall.com.